ACHIEVING SELF-COMPASSION

Giving Yourself the Gifts
of Happiness and Inner Peace

NATE TERRELL, LCSW

authorHOUSE®

AuthorHouse™
1663 Liberty Drive
Bloomington, IN 47403
www.authorhouse.com
Phone: 1 (800) 839-8640

Published by AuthorHouse 07/22/2016

ISBN: 978-1-5049-4901-9 (sc)
ISBN: 978-1-5049-4904-0 (e)

Library of Congress Control Number: 2015914948

Print information available on the last page.

ACKNOWLEDGMENTS

I am very excited to share with readers what I have learned about achieving self-compassion from both my personal and professional experiences.

Foremost, I want to thank my wife, Dr. Anita Foeman, for all her encouragement as I was writing this book. I also want to thank my son, Darqui, for inspiring me to write it and my daughter, Nikki, for helping me learn how to choose happiness and peace of mind, regardless of the challenges I face. Finally, I want to thank my clients who have taught me so much over the years about how self-compassion can promote healing and transform lives.

I also appreciate all of the support and feedback I have received from my many family members and friends who have read drafts of this book. Your help has been invaluable to me!

Contents

INTRODUCTION

The belief that "it is better to give than to receive" is a cornerstone of all major religions and an axiom that many of us learned at a young age and never questioned. Certainly, one of the most important things we can do with our lives is to help others and treat them with care and sensitivity. ·

However, our ability to meet the needs of others is largely contingent on our ability to treat *ourselves* with compassion. Our subsequent sense of happiness, inner peace and wholeness frees us to give to other people without depleting ourselves. Fortunately, we don't have to choose between being compassionate toward ourselves or others. We can do both at the same time and enjoy the rich fruits that both have to offer.

After reading earlier drafts of this book, a number of people have asked me if it's possible to have too much self-compassion. I responded that self-compassion is like love, kindness and good health - there is never too much. In fact, there is always room for more, just as with most of the best things in life.

Imagine that you have a very limited amount of food in your pantry. Now, visualize that your starving neighbor asks you for it. How can you give her your food without being unfair to yourself? Not only will you deplete your own dwindling supply, but you might build up some resentment towards her in the bargain.

In contrast, visualize that you have so much food it's spilling out of your doors and windows. Fruits, bread, vegetables and desserts - you've got an abundance of everything. Moreover, you have the resources to go back to the market any time to buy more. Now, you can give away a substantial amount of food to your neighbor without hurting yourself. In addition, you'll feel good about sharing what you have.

Compassion works the same way. When we fill ourselves up with it, we have plenty for others. In fact, the most generous people I know take such great care of themselves that they no longer experience an inner sense of scarcity. They are free to dedicate their lives to serving others while simultaneously practicing self-compassion and attentiveness to their own needs.

I wrote this book to enable you to experience the happiness and peace of mind that come from self-compassion and consequently expand your ability to be a resource to others. I have witnessed and experienced the effectiveness of the strategies I discuss during my many years of working with clients and my own quest to give myself the gift of self-compassion.

Chapter 1 offers a simple, vital strategy for achieving self-compassion that you can start practicing today. In Chapter 2, we explore commonly held beliefs that prevent you from living an effective life and how to change them. Chapter 3 discusses the fact that you are inherently worthy, regardless of how others perceive you or your faults. In Chapter 4, we focus on the importance of not projecting your needs onto others. Chapter 5 describes how a former client of mine overcame her depression and low self-worth by learning how to be more self-compassionate.

Chapter 6 focuses on how you can choose the gifts of happiness and peace of mind, regardless of the challenges you face. Chapter 7 is all about taking great care of yourself. In Chapter 8, you will learn how to get "out of your head" and "tune into" your deeper, authentic self. Chapter 9 tells you how you can eliminate negative reactions to difficult situations.

Chapter 10 encourages you to appreciate all you have so you can live your life with a sense of fulfillment rather than scarcity. In Chapter 11, you will discover a variety of portals to enjoy the wonders of the present moment. Finally, Chapter 12 concentrates on how your self-compassion enables you to experience an abundance of positive energy and caring that you can pass onto others.

My Evolution to Self-Compassion

My ability to treat myself with self-compassion has profoundly changed my life and enabled me to be more giving as a father, husband, friend, therapist, trainer, professor and citizen of this world. Now that I feel whole within myself, I do not project my needs as much onto others or live my life with a sense of inadequacy or lack. I also follow my inner voice that knows what I need to do at any moment to take great care of myself. Finally, I experience boundless inner peace as I "tune into" my authentic self, appreciating all I have and enjoying what each present moment has to offer.

I didn't start out this way. I grew up in a Quaker family in which my parents prioritized and modeled the importance of putting our needs aside to help others and work hard to create a better world. I vividly remember going with my mother to take clothes to the migrant farm workers who worked in the fields near our house in upstate New York, marching in Civil Rights demonstrations before I even understood why, receiving cash at Christmas that my father expected me to give away to some worthy cause and helping all of my friends solve their problems.

The underlying message was clear: the purpose of my life was to serve others. Not surprisingly, I received a Masters Degree in Social Work and began a 38-year career helping others, which has brought great meaning into my life and taught me invaluable lessons about how we can overcome challenges and grow into our best selves. Until recently, however, I never focused as much energy on being as good to myself as I did being good to others.

There were a number of reasons for this. First was my core belief that other people's needs were more important than my own and that I was responsible for meeting them. Secondly, I've always harbored a deep fear of appearing to be selfish or self-centered. Finally, I have a completely irrational desire for everyone to like me, which I worried might not happen if I focused on my own needs rather than the needs of others.

Although I take pride in my efforts to be helpful to others, the downside of this worldview is that I've often tried to do things for others that they did not want or need me to do. An excellent example of this concerns my 18-year-old son, Darqui, who experienced parental neglect and abuse before we adopted him at the age of nine. Although he is a "deep soul" who is generally very loving and positive, he was prone to angry moods when he first joined our family. Whenever he was in a negative frame of mind, I hovered around him, trying desperately to help him exorcise his inner demons and find happiness.

During a very difficult time in our relationship, Darqui informed me that he hated me for assuming that I knew how he should feel - he had the right to have a dark side and there was nothing I could ever do or say to help him feel any better. Jolted, I asked my son, "What can I do to help you?"

"Nothing," he snapped. "Worry about your own life."

He was so definitive that I had no choice but to respect his request. Although it was difficult, I ceased my efforts to change Darqui and reluctantly gave him the space he demanded. It was his life and I couldn't take away his pain and "make him" be happy regardless of how much I wanted to or loved him. In fact, I was contributing to his angst by acting like I could rescue him from himself.

After barely speaking to me for three months, he finally began to talk to me again. This time, I simply listened. When he again voiced any negative feelings, I nodded supportively and didn't try to change his perspective. As he talked, I also finally recognized how effective he was at getting to a better place all by himself, without any meddling on my part.

I now realize that it was grandiose for me to believe that I had the wisdom to understand and meet all the needs of Darqui - or anyone else, for that matter. Sure, I can listen carefully to others as they discuss their problems, offer whatever support and guidance I can muster and treat them with care and sensitivity. However, I am completely responsible for just one person's happiness - my own. This works out well because only I know on a deep level what I need to do to experience fulfillment, meaning, fun and all the other aspects of life that make it worth living. In fact, how could it possibly be otherwise? How would anyone else possibly know what I need to do in any given moment to feel good about myself or live the life I want?

The person who comes the closest to knowing is my wife, Anita. Although she has experienced me at my best and worst over the course of our long marriage and will do anything in her power to help me become my best self, there is simply no way she can ever identify more than a small fraction of my needs, much less figure out how to respond to them on a consistent basis. She can certainly listen to me when I am upset, encourage me to do the things that she knows bring me meaning and pleasure, provide me with useful feedback and leave me alone on Sunday afternoons in the fall to indulge my addiction to professional football. However, she can't make me happy even though

I unfairly used to long for her to do so. This is my task alone and one that I now heartily embrace.

Along with what I have learned experientially about achieving self-compassion, the privilege of helping my clients has also taught me a great deal about the most effective portals to self-compassion. Although I certainly focus on many other issues with clients, I have found that their deepest emotional pain is often caused by the harsh ways in which they speak to and judge themselves, their lack of self-worth and their inability to take effective care of themselves. I am honored to be their guide as they heal themselves by becoming more self-compassionate.

The power of self-compassion that I frequently observe within my clients has been validated by the research conducted by Dr. Kristin Neff, Associate Professor at the University of Texas, Austin. She and her colleague, Chris Germer (2013), found that study participants who were taught self-compassion techniques had less depression, anxiety, stress and emotional avoidance compared with a control group that did not receive the same training. The participants who received the training also had significantly higher levels of compassion for others and overall life satisfaction. Dr. Neff's groundbreaking research and writing is at the forefront of the growing self-compassion movement within the therapeutic community.

My only fear in writing this book is that the portals to achieve self-compassion that I discuss will appear to be overly simplistic to readers who are overwhelmed by the challenges they are facing in their lives. Without a doubt, self-compassion doesn't magically erase the pain of highly traumatic events or change difficult life circumstances. However, it does provide us with the positive energy and emotional boost we need to successfully weather the storms we encounter and empower us to change how we view and treat ourselves even if we can't change the world around us.

In fact, my clients always feel better about themselves and their lives as they let go of trying to govern what is beyond their domain and focus instead on becoming more self-compassionate, an act over which they have total control. This gives them the resilience they need to do what they can to overcome their challenges and to face their futures with a greater sense of hope and possibility.

I invite you also to experience the many benefits of self-compassion as you experiment with the strategies summarized at the end of each chapter to discover which ones work best for you. Like anything else, the more you practice being self-compassionate, the better you will be at it.

Chapter 1
BE YOUR OWN BEST FRIEND

In this book, you will learn many strategies and exercises to enable you to achieve self-compassion. But in my experience, the quickest and easiest way to succeed in this compelling endeavor is simply to change the way you talk to yourself.

Unfortunately, many people beat themselves up in a harsh, judgmental manner that drains their spirit and creates self-doubt. For instance, when they make a mistake, they might say to themselves, "You never do anything right" or "You are such a loser." In fact, self-torment is a major cause of depression and even despair.

In stark contrast, it is highly self-compassionate to speak to yourself inside your head or out loud in a calm, caring and helpful manner, just like you are your own best friend. For instance, you might say to yourself during a hard time, "Hang in there. I am behind you all the way," or "Just do the best you can." You can begin this practice immediately and carry out this simple strategy anywhere and at any time, entirely free of charge.

The beauty of this portal into self-compassion is that only *we* know exactly what we need to hear to feel better about ourselves in a low moment or to gather the courage we need to face a difficult challenge. Rather than spending our lives searching for people who are able to tell us exactly what we need to hear to feel good about ourselves or to fill up our internal holes, we can accomplish these things simply through the loving and supportive messages we give ourselves. As a result, we can enjoy our relationships with others without the erroneous expectation that they are responsible for making us happy or healing our emotional wounds.

I prefer to talk to myself out loud because it adds validity and emphasis to what I am saying. My favorite place for this activity is in the car, where I have privacy and little else to do besides driving safely. I also often talk to myself in the shower as I gear up for each day, which provides me with uncanny wisdom and problem-solving ability. Perhaps I am trying to cleanse my psyche as well as my body.

1

One of the most important times to be my own best friend is when I fail to live up to my own - or other people's - expectations. Rather than beat myself up with critical naysaying, I will say something out loud to myself, such as, "OK buddy, you messed up, but I love you anyway. Just make sure that you never do it again." This does not prevent me from doing whatever I need to do to fix a problem or repairing a relationship tear I have caused. In fact, my ability to be gentle with myself helps me think clearly through my options and arrive at the best one rather than wallowing in self-criticism.

I also talk to myself like I am my own best friend about painful past experiences and aspects of myself that I'm not comfortable discussing with others. My own soothing words reassure me that I can have compassion for myself even in the midst of feelings of regret or shame. Only I know the darkest corners of my soul and can free myself from the power they have over me through self-love and forgiveness. These corners grow bigger and more toxic when we allow them to fester; they dissipate when exposed to the light of self-compassion.

Finally, I talk to myself supportively about new things I want to try, changes I want to make, aspects of myself I feel good about, pleasant memories and anything else that enables me to feel happy and vital about my life. When I am doing something alone, I will often comment to myself how much I am enjoying it. In fact, I sometimes provide myself with ongoing commentary throughout the day, complete with astute observations, inside jokes and encouraging remarks. I also write friendly e-mails to myself or leave positive messages on my desk that I will see when I get home after a hectic day.

My ability to be my own best friend allows me to enjoy dates with myself. For example, every Thursday I take myself out to lunch between the classes on Interpersonal Communication that I teach at Temple University. The serenity I experience as I relish my food and roam around in my inner world is a welcome respite from the intensity of classroom teaching and helps me maintain my peaceful center. When my date goes well, as it always does, I never forget to say to myself, "Thanks, buddy, I had a great time."

I have learned experientially that a major key to happiness is to take advantage of every possible opportunity to be my own best friend. As I have focused intently on this goal in the last couple of years, it has become more than a compelling habit - it's a way of being. This provides me with a protective balm against the unpredictable shifts of life and enables me to respond with an internal sense of perspective and calm.

One of the key benefits of talking to ourselves in a compassionate manner is the power it gives us to respond effectively to significant challenges. Clearly, when we are faced with a dangerous or highly traumatic situation, the fight-or-flight part of our brain, called the amygdala, activates our limbic system and usually causes us to experience some level of stress. However, I have found that even in the most difficult circumstances, it's possible to talk to myself in a way that brings me greater emotional balance.

For example, on a hot summer evening a few years ago, I received a phone call from a nurse who told me that my mother had experienced a serious stroke at the facility where she lived. Initially, I felt a sense of panic as my thoughts raced to whether I would ever see her alive again. Fortunately, I remembered to consult my "best friend" and began to talk to myself in such a caring and soothing way on the drive to the hospital that I experienced an almost eerie sense of calm. When I arrived, I was able to keep my fear and worry at bay and be totally emotionally present with my mother. I sat by her bedside all night holding her hand, talking about happy family memories and telling her how much I loved her.

Think about it: we spend all of our time inside of ourselves. The contrast between the quality of life of people who are their own best friend and those who constantly beat themselves up is immeasurable over the course of a lifetime. Although we generally don't have control over what happens around us, we alone regulate how we talk to ourselves and this choice largely determines our level of happiness and well-being.

Imagine if everyone was their own best friend and therefore happy within themselves. Since most destructive behaviors are caused by unhappiness, the world would be a much more peaceful community and we would all treat each other with greater kindness and caring. Each of us can begin to create this world of goodwill - one self-compassionate statement at a time.

<u>Try These Strategies on for Size</u>

> ➤ Talk to yourself inside your head or out loud in a caring, calm and helpful manner, just like you are your own best friend.
> ➤ If you do not feel good about yourself, focus particularly on what you need to say to yourself to feel better and counter negative messages you give to yourself and/or receive from others.
> ➤ Recognize that only you know what you want to hear at any given moment.
> ➤ Talk with yourself in a compassionate and understanding manner about aspects of yourself or your life that you aren't comfortable sharing with others.
> ➤ Go out on dates with just yourself to do the things you most enjoy in the company of someone you love (hopefully). Without any social responsibilities, you are free to focus on simply basking in the pleasures and meaning each moment brings.
> ➤ Know that you have the ability to respond more effectively to difficult situations by changing how you talk to yourself.

Chapter 2
DEVELOP BELIEFS THAT WORK FOR YOU

Each of us holds a set of beliefs about ourselves, other people and the world around us. We develop these tenets from the messages we received from our parents and other significant people in our lives, society at large and our own experiences. They form the framework of our lives and largely determine our thoughts, feelings and behavior.

Therefore, one of the keys to self-compassion is to assess how well any given belief is working for us in our efforts to live fulfilling and effective lives. If a belief is not serving us well, we can choose to replace it with a more functional one, like we are shedding an old skin. Unfortunately, many people never question the validity of their beliefs and continue to hold on to perspectives that are self-defeating.

A key component of my work with clients is to collaboratively identify the underlying beliefs that are not working for them. I then encourage them to discard them by visualizing that they are cutting a string between themselves and their dysfunctional beliefs with a sword. Finally, I help my clients identify more functional beliefs and encourage them to "try them on" to see how well they work.

During our next session, we discuss the impact that their new beliefs are having on their lives and if they need to be further modified to achieve better results. Although the process of belief change often appears daunting to my clients, I encourage them to view it as an experiment in the process of becoming their best selves. The realization that they have the capacity to choose new beliefs often provides them with a crucial sense of hope and is a key step in their efforts to overcome their problems and enjoy greater happiness and inner peace in their lives.

I often help my clients focus on the beliefs they most need to replace by asking them to remember a recent time when they behaved in a manner that was reactive or irrational. I then help them identify and change the underlying dysfunctional notions that led to this behavior. The effectiveness of their new beliefs is evident as they begin to respond to similar situations in a more functional way.

For instance, I had a client named Steve (all the names of clients I use in this book have been changed to protect their confidentiality) who believed that he could get his wife to treat him better by yelling at her. Not surprisingly, his behavior did not motivate her to change and only led to frequent shouting matches and increasing marital discord. After much discussion, Steve recognized that he needed to be the change he wanted in his marriage by talking with her in a calm manner and treating her with more love and sensitivity. He was surprised at how quickly she began to return the favor and their marriage improved dramatically.

I often give my clients a list of beliefs that commonly lead to unhappiness and a second list of beliefs that lead to happiness. I then ask them to identify the beliefs they hold from each list that they would like to eliminate or "try on." I upgrade this list as I gain a better understanding of the impact that various beliefs have on the lives of my clients. I also enjoy the opportunity to talk with happy people about what they believe since this gives me new ideas about how to improve my list of helpful beliefs.

Although it takes a while for my clients to fully adopt a new belief, even small shifts in their thought process enable them to achieve greater happiness and inner peace. This provides the motivation they need to continue their process of belief change, which gains momentum like a snowball rolling down a hill. As clients discover that they have the ability to significantly change their lives simply by changing their beliefs, they experience an expanding sense of empowerment and emotional freedom.

Some clients feel ungrounded or adrift between the time they discard an old belief and replace it with a more effective one. I assure them that what they are experiencing during this liminal period in their lives is a normal reaction to moving from the known to the unknown and that it dissipates as they begin to consolidate new perspectives into their worldview. They just need to hang in there until they land in a better place.

Do Not Allow Others to Define You

One common dysfunctional belief is that our lovability and worth are determined by the messages and treatment we receive from others. Consequently, our self-esteem goes up and down like a bouncing ball we have no control over. When we are given a compliment, we feel terrific, but when we are criticized or ignored by others, our confidence plummets. This gives others a great deal of power over us and makes it easier for them to manipulate us into being the person they want us to be.

When we feel good about ourselves regardless of how others respond to us, we are happier and more centered. This does not mean that we should ignore helpful feedback from others. If several people tell you that your sarcasm is hurtful, you have a responsibility to eliminate your unkind behavior. However, you do not need to feel badly about yourself to do so. If fact, if you allow critical feedback to torpedo your self-esteem, you are less likely to have the energy you need to change.

It is important to recognize that the messages we receive from others usually tell us more about who *they* are than who *we* are. Their reaction to us is a reflection of their own opinions, values and personal "triggers" rather than an indictment of who we are. For instance, if you tell your family members and friends that you are going to quit your job and cross the Atlantic Ocean in a 36-foot sailboat, your adventurous relatives and friends will probably cheer you on, whereas the more cautious folks will likely discourage you. Clearly, these different reactions do not define you - how can they, since they are diametrically opposed? They simply help you better understand your family and friends.

Highly successful people maintain their self-esteem regardless of how they are treated and weigh the feedback they receive carefully. If it is useful, they incorporate it. If it is not useful, they ignore it. These individuals have the wisdom to not allow others to determine who they are and value what they think more than the opinions of others.

Basing one's self-esteem on the reaction of another person is also taxing on relationships. A few years ago, I worked with Megan and Alex, a couple whose marriage was in deep distress. Megan grew up in a highly affectionate and emotionally expressive family, which led her to believe that her lovability was measured by how emotionally demonstrative Alex was towards her. In contrast, Alex grew up with overly critical parents who rarely expressed emotions. Consequently, he felt deeply uncomfortable in emotionally intense situations and protected himself by withdrawing into the safety of his own world.

These dynamics unfortunately caused both Megan and Alex to feel badly about themselves. When Megan became highly emotional, Alex felt overwhelmed and withdrew from her. This left Megan feeling as though her husband didn't love her or find her attractive. In turn, the subsequent hurt she experienced left Alex feeling that he was not an adequate husband.

Alex's behavior had nothing to do with how he felt about his wife - in truth, he loved her very much - but was simply a reflection of his own way of coping. Megan's eventual recognition of this enabled her to feel good about herself regardless of how he responded to her. For his part, Alex recognized that Megan loved him unconditionally and that he, therefore, did not need to protect himself from her like he did with his judgmental parents. Consequently, he was able to remain more emotionally present with her when she was upset.

The Perfection Trap

A second troublesome belief that many of us hold is that we must be perfect at all times. Consequently, we put ourselves down whenever we make a mistake, which drains our energy and often leads to a sense of defeat or even depression. We also avoid taking on challenges that, if achieved, might significantly improve our lives because we fear falling short.

What if we choose to believe, instead, that errors are inevitable and can teach us useful life lessons? The wisest among us do not dread mistakes, but rather welcome them as a gift. They allow us to continue to gain self-knowledge and wisdom, which actually helps us to avoid future missteps.

When you think about it, the notion that we can be perfect if we just try hard enough is grandiose. It would mean that we had achieved something that no one has ever accomplished before. Although it might be quite satisfying to be the first human being to achieve perfection, it certainly would not endear us to others, who would likely feel highly inadequate in our presence. Our unique status would also be very difficult to maintain, especially as we encounter old age.

One of the major benefits of shedding our need to be perfect is that it enables us to share our fears and vulnerabilities with others who give us the caring and support we need to overcome them. In fact, as we recognize that the most important people in our lives continue to love and value us despite our imperfections, we are able to connect with them on increasingly deeper levels. We owe it to ourselves to seek out friends, romantic partners, family members and/or therapists who unconditionally accept all aspects of who we are. While in their presence, we are free to let down our guard and achieve a level of radical honestly, which opens up new possibilities for healing and growth.

Perhaps the biggest challenge is to open up to others about aspects of ourselves about which we feel ashamed. The terror of humiliation is hardwired into us: the most common dream in the world is to find ourselves naked in a public setting. Consequently, we often lock our most painful secrets in an internal vault to protect us from the judgments of others. However, this vault does not defend us from our own self-judgments, which usually cause our greatest emotional pain and haunt us in insidious and self-destructive ways.

We can free ourselves of the toxic impact of internalized shame by being kind to ourselves even in the midst of our imperfections. This certainly does not give us license to mistreat others or absolve us of the need to accept responsibility for our actions, which is part of the glue that holds a civil society together. It simply enables us to be more self-compassionate and use the energy we have wasted feeling badly about ourselves to take better care of ourselves and others.

In an environment of trust, sharing our experiences of shame with others can be liberating. For example, I was a member of a men's group for many years where we talked honestly about our lives and supported each other in becoming our best selves. After we had gotten to know each other very well, we decided to each share the aspect of ourselves that we felt the most shame about. I clearly remember how freeing it was for me to discuss a previously hidden and painful facet of myself with my fellow group members who did not judge me. In fact, they were puzzled that I felt any shame about this part of me.

It has always interested me that when people introduce themselves at Alcoholics Anonymous meetings, they say their name and then note that they are an alcoholic. By allowing themselves to be publically vulnerable in front of people they may have never met before, they are exorcising their shame and inviting others to join them in this process, therefore building the sense of community and mutual trust that makes AA an effective self-help movement.

One of the benefits of treating ourselves with self-compassion regardless of our faults is that it makes it much easier to acknowledge mistakes we have made. This is because our sense of worth is not threatened when we admit our imperfections and we consequently do not experience emotional pain. In contrast, people who lack self-compassion and consequently feel unworthy usually have a difficult time admitting their mistakes because it is too painful and threatens their fragile sense of self. This significantly impairs their ability to make positive changes and damages their relationships.

I see the healing power of this process with the couples who come to me for therapy. When clients refuse to acknowledge their piece of a conflict, it usually drives their partner to be equally righteous and creates an escalating and unwinnable power struggle between them. However, when one member of a couple acknowledges his or her part, the partner almost always does the same because an opening for healing has been created. As this process gains momentum, their increasing trust and goodwill enables them to solve their conflicts, often without any additional guidance from me.

It's a funny thing: we tend to fear that others will think less of us for admitting our mistakes, yet the opposite is generally true. When people take responsibility for what they have done wrong, our respect for them usually increases. When they pass the buck, we usually respect them less. I feel sorry for people who are unable to ever admit they were wrong because it is exhausting to convince others that we are always right and displays an arrogance that often drives people away.

The link between sharing vulnerability and deepening interpersonal connection extends to many kinds of relationships. Although I am careful about sharing personal information with my clients, I find that our therapeutic bond is often strengthened when I acknowledge my own imperfections and how I have tried to correct them. For instance, when I'm working with clients who have problems controlling their anger, I share that I once had a very quick temper and would yell at family members during arguments. I go on to tell these clients how I have learned to curb my temper by changing the thoughts and beliefs that fuel my anger and using visualizations that enable me to respond to challenging situations more calmly and constructively.

Along with giving clients concrete strategies they can use, my self-disclosure often helps them feel more comfortable opening up and discussing their vulnerabilities with me. In fact, I am surprised by how often clients tell me at the end of our work together that they benefited from hearing a bit about the struggles I have faced in my own life. The key, of course, is to always keep our focus on their issues and needs rather than mine.

Let Go of What is Beyond Your Control

A third belief that causes people to experience high levels of stress and frustration is that they should be in control at all times. It is only natural that we want to maintain as much control as we can over the course of our lives, how we treat others and what we do to be healthy. However, when we try to change what is beyond our domain, such as how other people behave or the way the events in our lives turn out, we are setting ourselves up for disappointment.

People often become overly controlling in an attempt to quell their internal anxiety or chaos. They seek an outer certainty to compensate for their internal uncertainty. When their efforts to control the world around them inevitably fail, they often become even more controlling because they are still operating under an erroneous belief system. However, if they have the wisdom to let go of what is beyond their control, they are free to focus on what they *can do* to experience more inner peace, such as being more self-compassionate.

Many of the best things that have ever happened to me have occurred because I let go of something I was trying to control that I couldn't. My marriage improved significantly when I began to accept Anita as she was rather than expecting her to share my emotional intensity or love of being in the woods. My relationship with Darqui grew stronger when I began to trust him to find his own happiness rather than making the mistake of believing I could make him happy. My level of inner peace increased when I gave up the need for others to share my political and social opinions, which has not prevented me from speaking out about what I believe is right.

One of the most important things we need to let go of is our vision for how our children should be. Although it is certainly appropriate for us to guide our kids towards good values, safety and eventual self-sufficiency (if possible), it is not fair to expect them to be scholars if they have significant learning challenges or the social butterfly we were in high school if they would rather curl up with a good book than go to a party. In fact, our ability to unconditionally accept our children as they are is probably the greatest gift we can ever give them.

We also give ourselves a gift when we celebrate our children rather than try to control them because they are then open to what we want to teach them, enjoy being with us rather than avoid us out of self-protection and have no need to rebel against us. Young people have a very acute ability to sense whether their parents accept them unconditionally, and they give back in droves to those who measure up. In contrast, children who do not receive validation from their parents often resent them and become self-centered in an effort to provide for themselves.

As my clients differentiate between what they can and can't control, they are free to focus their energies on what they can do to live the lives they want. They experience a sense of liberation and serenity as they let go of what is beyond their domain. In fact, their ability to be happy and achieve their goals is usually based on their ability to accept rather than fight what they are unable to change or control.

You Are Not Alone in Your Problems

A fourth unhelpful belief is that we are all alone in our problems and that everyone else has an easier time of it. Yet every human being who has ever lived has grappled with similar challenges such as stress, depression, anxiety, disappointment, sickness or the loss of a loved one. Therefore, one of the most self-compassionate things we can do is recognize that the difficulties we encounter are by no means unique to us. This realization reduces our sense of isolation from others and enables us to feel a deeper connection to all of humanity.

We can deepen this connection by seeking out others who face similar life situations. For example, I attended a support group for fathers of children with special needs for many years and felt very much at home as we discussed our common challenges and joys within an environment of mutual understanding and trust. I particularly relished being with others who were equally offended by words such as stupid and idiot, which convey the prejudice that exists in our society towards people with cognitive challenges like my daughter, Nikki, who you will read about later on in this book.

A client of mine named Jennifer suffered from very low self-esteem and told me that when sitting amidst a huge crowd at a baseball game, she still felt very alone due to her belief that she was the only one there with problems. I encouraged her to recognize that everyone at the game had something difficult they were grappling with and visualize that this connected her to them like drops of water are connected to the ocean. Jennifer began to practice this new perspective whenever she was in a crowd of people, which significantly reduced her sense of isolation and enabled her to feel better about herself and her life.

Changing the Wrong Person

A fifth ineffective belief is that other people have to behave a certain way for us to be happy. For example, my father tried to mold my mother into the person he wanted her to be by frequently telling her how unhappy he was about all of the ways she did not measure up to his expectations. Rather than being motivated to make changes, my mother just grew to resent him and expressed her anger in passive-aggressive ways. Of course, she could never have lived up to my father's image of the perfect wife, even if she'd spent every ounce of her energy on this task, because she was a flesh-and-blood, fallible human being rather than a figment of my father's imagination.

This is not to suggest that we don't have the right to request that other people stop treating us unfairly or behaving in ways that are destructive. However, if we base our happiness on our need for others to be a certain way, we are likely to always be frustrated. The only person we can change is, of course, ourselves. In fact, I've never had a relationship problem that I couldn't improve by changing something about myself.

It is clearly more effective to believe that we can help others succeed in making reasonable changes (especially if they want to), but these changes do not have to occur for us to be happy. To believe otherwise gives others way too much power over us. It also takes up energy we could use to create the lives we want - a much more achievable goal!

Avoid a Victim Mentality

A final commonly-held dysfunctional belief is that "I am a victim." In the short run, this conviction may make us feel powerful because it gets us attention and compels others to try to help us. However, in the long run, it drains our spirit and blocks our motivation to improve our lives. It also eventually drives away other people, who become frustrated and exhausted by the inertia of our victim mentality.

The only way I have been able to help clients let go of their victimhood is to point out how self-destructive it is and ask them how well this viewpoint is working for them. If they are motivated to let it go, I provide them with the support they need to heal from actual experiences of victimization all the while encouraging them to not overgeneralize or allow these experiences to define their identity. I also help them feel empowered by recognizing that they always have options, even if all they can do is shift their perspective on a situation they are unable to change.

I am always inspired when I encounter people who have experienced significant life challenges, but have not developed a victim mentality. One of these people is Dr. Daniel Gottlieb, a Philadelphia psychologist who was paralyzed from the neck down in his early adulthood when a tire flew off a truck and smashed into his car. Rather than view himself as a victim, he has spent his professional career helping countless others through his clinical work, radio show, public talks and numerous books.

I recently had the pleasure of hearing Dr. Gottlieb speak. He began by talking about all of the things he valued in his life. He went on to tell many stories about how the power of love enabled him to overcome the many difficulties he had grappled with and be helpful to others. However, it was not his words that touched me on such a deep level. It was the pure love that radiated from every cell in his body and left me with a glow that lasted for a long time.

My Own Challenges

The belief that has been the hardest for me to let go is that I am somehow responsible for the negative feelings of those around me and consequently need to help anyone who appears unhappy to become happier. Although I recognize that this conviction originated during my childhood when I felt responsible for helping my depressed mother, it is rooted deeply within my psyche and has felt as much a part of me as my nose does for most of my life.

However, after many years of allowing the burdens of others to impair my happiness, I have finally recognized that I am not responsible for the upset feelings of anyone else as long as I did not do anything to cause these sentiments. As a result, I am able to maintain an inner sense of happiness and peace, even if those around me are distraught. This realization hasn't reduced my empathy for other people or hindered my ability to be a resource to them if they are open to my help. I actually have more energy to give to others because I am no longer weighed down by any negative emotions they may be experiencing.

This new belief has helped me be a more effective resource to my wife, Anita, when she is stressed. In the past, I would absorb her emotional pain and consequently respond to whatever issues she was discussing with my own frustration. It was sometimes difficult for me to listen carefully to her because I was caught up in my personal reactions. Now that I do not take on whatever emotions she is feeling, I maintain my emotional balance and am free to respond effectively to her needs rather than my own.

I have also labored under the erroneous belief for most of my life that I need to be liked by everyone. Consequently, when I sensed that someone did not like me, I tried to "win them over" by changing myself into who I thought I needed to be to gain their approval. Not only did this never work, it was also exhausting and left me feeling inauthentic and vulnerable.

I have finally recognized that some people are not going to like or understand me, regardless of how I try to contort myself. Rather than waste my energy swimming against the tide, I now maximize the time I spend with the people with whom I feel the most comfortable, and I steer clear of those with whom I am unable to connect. I subscribe to Robert Fulghum's perspective, which he wrote about in his book, *True Love,* "We are all a little weird. And life is a little weird. And when we find someone whose weirdness is compatible with ours, we join up with them and fall into mutually satisfying weirdness - and call it love - true love."

Occasionally, however, I feel let down by everyone or that no one really "gets me." When this occurs, I say to myself, "the heck with everyone" and retreat to my beloved, family cabin in the beautiful and serene Pine Barrens of New Jersey to lick my wounds. There, I'm never lonely because I am with my best friend who understands me deeply, is devoted to my happiness, does an excellent job of meeting my needs and is always on my side. After a couple of hours of solitude, I am ready to re-enter the outside world with a lighter spirit and sense of renewal.

The process of belief change is not as easy as flipping a light switch - it takes a good deal of focus and commitment. However, the simple recognition that an underlying tenet is not working loosens the grip it has over us and opens us up to more effective ways of viewing ourselves and the world around us. Consequently, we experience an increased sense of control over our lives and an emotional lift as the negative thoughts and feelings created by our erroneous beliefs dissipate.

People often comment to me that it is tough for them to change their beliefs. I respond that it is probably harder for them to maintain beliefs that are making their lives difficult out of habit or fear of change than it is to develop more functional ones. Without a doubt, one of the best things about life is that we have the ability to change our beliefs whenever we need to do so. This gives me a profound sense of freedom and leaves me feeling like an eagle soaring high in the sky.

One of my deepest satisfactions is seeing my clients successfully "try on" a new belief to see how well it fits. Although ideally I guide my clients through the process of identifying and replacing their ineffective beliefs with ones that work better for them, some are unable to recognize beliefs that are making their lives more difficult, much less figure out how to replace them. When this is the case, I am highly directive in pointing out their destructive beliefs and suggesting alternatives.

For instance, I once worked with a young woman who had suffered from debilitating depression since her childhood. Karen believed that she needed to figure out why she was so depressed before she could feel better and had spent years in therapy trying to achieve this goal to no avail. Early on in our work together, I pointed out to her that this perspective did not appear to be working for her and suggested that she replace it with the conviction that self-compassion, rather than insight, would help her break free from her depression.

Although puzzled by this new concept, Karen agreed to give it a try. Subsequently, we began to focus on what she could do to take better care of herself, detach from family members who put her down for being too serious and find people who accepted her for who she was. Finally freed from her belief that insight had to precede action, she made remarkable progress and soon began to feel much happier about herself and her life.

Try These Strategies on for Size

> ➢ Identify your core beliefs about yourself, others or the world at large and assess how well each one is working for you.
> ➢ If a given belief is not working, visualize that there is a string between yourself and your belief and cut it.
> ➢ Replace dysfunctional beliefs with ones that you think may work better for you and "try them on" to see if they help you live a more effective, happier and peaceful life.
> ➢ Recognize that you always have the ability to change your beliefs even if all you can do is shift your perspective on a situation that you are unable to change.
> ➢ Know that it is easier to replace a belief that is not working than it is to hold onto it out of habit or fear of change.

Chapter 3
KNOW YOU ARE INHERENTLY WORTHY

Although the unhelpful beliefs discussed in the last chapter certainly create unhappiness, the most toxic tenet that many people hold is that they are unworthy. This is usually because their parents or caretakers acted as if they were not lovable or important during their formative years. As a result, they developed the perception that something was significantly wrong with them, failing to realize that the bad treatment they received was caused by their parent's unhappiness, emotional limitations, etc. rather than their unworthiness.

Imagine that a 5-year-old boy is sitting on the living room couch watching cartoons when his mother comes home from work. She yells at him to turn the television down and then completely ignores him for the rest of the evening. It is very unlikely that he is able to think to himself, "I am lovable and worthy regardless of how my mother treats me. She is just stressed out." More likely, he assumes that there is something wrong with him and that he therefore deserves the treatment he is receiving. Otherwise, why would this powerful person in his life treat him the way she did? Perhaps he even acts out at bedtime to confirm the negative identity he has begun to develop, which leaves him feeling even worse about himself.

On a more personal note, Darqui was drowning in his negative view of himself when he first joined our family, caused by the bad treatment he had received from his biological mother and previous foster parents. In fact, he had only been at our house for a few hours when he flung himself across his bed, buried his face in his pillow and shouted, "I am a loser" over and over again. I vividly remember his response to me as I stood over him and lovingly informed him he was perfect just as he was. He looked up at me tentatively and asked with bewilderment and hope, "Really?"

"Absolutely," I replied and thus launched him on his journey from despair to worthiness.

People also feel unworthy because they do not live up to the expectations they have for themselves, or that others have for them, concerning their physical appearance, professional success, economic status, and so on. They believe that they need to "earn" their worth by meeting these expectations and mistakenly determine that feeling unworthy will somehow propel them to become the people they want to be. However, their sense of unworthiness drains their spirit and decreases their ability to make positive changes in their lives, creating a toxic downward spiral of self-castigation, depression and lethargy.

When we view ourselves as unworthy, we live our lives in fear that others will discover how deeply flawed we are. We are also at high risk for engaging in self-destructive behaviors, such as addictions, that numb our pain and only increase our fundamental sense of inadequacy. We don't realize that our insidious "unworthiness" exists solely within our imaginations. It's a belief, not a fact. And we alone have the power to change it.

Our unworthiness is often compounded by our assumption that we don't deserve the support and love we receive from others. We lock ourselves in a self-created and barren emotional prison, blocking the very warmth and light we crave to feel better about ourselves. We do not realize that one of the most compassionate things we can do for ourselves and those who care for us is to take in, rather than reject, the caring we are given.

It is often said that it is impossible to love others unless you love yourself. However, I do not believe this is the case. I have known many people, including most of my clients, who are giving to others, but not to themselves. They provide other people with the caring they long for themselves, perhaps with the hope that it will somehow be reflected back to them. When I ask them if they believe everyone should be treated with compassion, they always respond affirmatively. I then point out that they are included in everyone and encourage them to give themselves the same care and kindness that they so generously provide to others.

You Are Inherently Worthy

I have found that one of the most effective ways to help clients with low self-worth climb out of their self-defeating emotional quagmire is to tell them flat out: "You are inherently worthy and lovable, regardless of how others have treated you or your life experiences." I then encourage them to "try on" this new belief until we meet again. Although it often strikes them as difficult, simply entertaining this possibility creates a small crack in their previously unchallenged negative view of themselves. This is generally the beginning of the healing process.

My conviction that my clients are worthy is based on my Quaker belief that every human being has an "inner light" that can never be extinguished. This light is the source of our best qualities, such as kindness, goodwill and forgiveness. Although self-serving and destructive people are certainly less valuable to society than those who are giving and loving, their behavior stems from their lack of empathy, arrogance, emotional wounds and dysfunctional beliefs rather than their lack of an "inner light." They are still worthy and possess the capacity to have a more positive impact on the world if they are able to connect with this light and allow it to inspire them to be more caring human beings.

Although I rarely share my spiritual beliefs with my clients, I do provide them with the support and guidance they need to recognize their inherent worth, eliminate anything they are doing that is destructive to themselves or others and become their best selves. Perhaps the most rewarding aspect of my therapeutic work is that it enables me to be a guide and companion to my clients during this exciting time of healing and growth in their lives.

I once worked with a 15-year-old boy named Larry who had been referred to me from his school for drawing racist images in his notebook. In fact, his mother reported that he could not return to school until school officials received a letter from me stating that he had overcome his prejudices. During the course of our work together, it became evident that his inappropriate behavior stemmed from the fact that he felt deeply inadequate due to his very demanding father, who constantly criticized him, and the bullying he received from classmates because he worked on his family farm. His racist drawings were an attempt to make him feel superior to others and consequently build his sense of worth.

However, the lift Larry received from these drawings never lasted and, in fact, only made him feel worse, just as drinking salt water intensifies thirst. After a great deal of discussion, he was able to shift his beliefs and recognize that the behavior of his father and the bullies who tormented him stemmed from their insensitivity and was not a reflection of his worth. He also realized that his racist drawings resulted from his anger and emotional pain rather than his true being.

As he began to feel better about himself, Larry let go of his prejudices and became a more caring and happier person. He continued with therapy beyond the sessions he was required to attend and I am grateful for the lessons he taught me about the origins of racist behavior and how it can be overcome. I am also glad that I had the opportunity to help him find his "inner light" through the compassion I gave to him.

Self-Worth vs. Narcissism

It is important to note that there is a huge difference between self-worth and narcissism, which I certainly do not want to help clients develop since it is based on the assumption that one is superior to others and it causes people to be selfish and arrogant. In fact, narcissistic people lack the empathy they need to be caring human beings and constantly need to judge and put others down to reinforce their own false sense of betterment.

The momentary boost that narcissistic people derive from feeling better than others soon disappears, forcing them to be even more judgmental, which impairs their relationships. In contrast, when people build their worth through self-compassion, they are able to recognize the fundamental value of others even if they do not like specific things about them.

Unlike narcissism, self-worth is simply feeling good about and unconditionally accepting ourselves as we are. It is not something we earn through our wealth, accomplishments, good looks or erroneous belief that we have more value than others. Rather, it is a gift we can give to ourselves that can't be taken away by anyone except ourselves.

When we experience self-worth, we are able to see the best rather than the worst in others. Consequently, we develop a much more positive and hopeful worldview. In addition, others are attracted to us because they know we will accept them for who they are and hope our inner peace and happiness will rub off onto them. Finally, we have the ability to accept negative feedback and use it to improve ourselves in contrast to narcissistic people who reject feedback and consequently remain stagnant.

Beliefs that Undermine Self-Worth

Some of my clients are afraid to give themselves the gift of self-worth because they fear it will cause them to become self-centered. I point out that the opposite is true. Unhappy people who do not like themselves are understandably self-centered in their perpetual quest to eliminate their inner demons and gain some relief from their misery.

In contrast, people who feel worthy and whole within have no need to be self-centered and can instead turn their energies to caring for others and doing their part to build a better world. They are able to enjoy the rewards of being compassionate to others while simultaneously taking great care of themselves since these compelling ideals are not mutually exclusive. To me, this is the essence of a well-lived life!

You may also hesitate to let go of your negative view of yourself because you assume that your low self-worth will compel you to overcome your faults and become the person you long to be. In my experience, it rarely works this way. People who feel badly about themselves simply don't have the energy or confidence to pursue self-growth. Rather than feel empowered, they usually remain stuck in their inertia and unhappiness.

For example, people who want to lose weight often judge themselves harshly and then overeat in an attempt to feel better. Afterward, they may feel ashamed of their behavior and even more down on themselves - feelings they bury by eating still more. I encourage clients who are trapped in this cycle to start by totally accepting themselves as they are. This eliminates the sense of inadequacy that so often causes unhealthy eating habits and also gives them the emotional lift they need to take better care of themselves. Many of my clients are pleased to find that their extra pounds drop off as they eliminate their negative self-judgments and practice greater self-compassion.

I once worked with a client who told me that she thought she could rid herself of her self-hatred if she just felt badly enough about herself. Consequently, she frequently berated herself for all the mistakes she had made, her inability to find a job and the fact that she was still financially dependent on her family. Needless to say, her self-castigation caused her to feel even worse rather than eliminating the negative feelings she had about herself.

Some people also believe that their low self-worth acts as a protector. Their logic goes like this: if they beat themselves up enough, no one else will have the power to bring them down. However, the opposite is true. The bullies of the world have an uncanny ability to pick out people who do not like themselves, and delight in wounding them further. The reaction of fear and hurt that bullies receive from their victims only serves to scratch their itch for power, control or simply attention, which leads them to continue their destructive behavior.

By contrast, bullies get no satisfaction from trying to torment people who feel good about themselves, because they don't get the reaction they crave. Trying to bully a person with strong self-worth is like boxing alone - all you encounter is air. In fact, when I conduct anti-bullying training in schools, bullies often tell me that harassing people who like themselves is "no fun."

It is an unfortunate fact that people generally treat us as we treat ourselves. If we act like we are worthy, others assume this to be the case and respond to us with respect and perhaps even deference. In contrast, if we act as if we are deeply flawed, others assume we do not deserve good treatment and respond accordingly. This creates a tragic downward spiral that only ends when we begin to love ourselves as we are.

Finally, many people feel that they deserve low self-worth because of the mistakes they have made or because they haven't lived up to their own or others' expectations. They believe they need to punish themselves and/or become better people before they deserve to feel good about who they are.

Let's look more closely at this. First, your negative feelings about yourself can't erase your mistakes. Furthermore, everybody makes blunders - it's part of being human. Self-worth is not a prize to be earned from living the perfect life, but rather it is a gift we can always give to ourselves, regardless of our inevitable failings. When we forgive ourselves for our faults, we have more energy to focus on becoming our best selves.

Benefits of "Trying On" Self-Worth

After my clients begin to understand that low self-worth does not serve them in any way, they are almost always open to "trying on" the belief that they are worthy. Although they rarely come into the following session bursting with self-confidence, they almost always report that they have enjoyed at least some relief from their unhappiness. It's as if they have been sitting in a dark room all of their lives and cracked open the door, letting in a welcome sliver of light.

As my clients begin to feel more worthy and shed their old "skin" of self-criticism and inadequacy, they are more motivated and energized to improve their lives and achieve their goals. Our work then turns to how they can open this door wider through self-compassion and effective self-care. Rather than becoming more self-centered, they are now better able to focus on the needs of others even as they take better care of themselves. As they are filled up with happiness, it is only natural that they want to spread it around, which, in turn, increases their happiness. It is a cycle of increasing abundance.

I also encourage clients to never compare themselves negatively to others. Doing so sinks their sense of worth like a brick thrown into a pond and rarely inspires them to make positive changes in their lives. In fact, whenever I make the mistake of thinking that someone else is better than me in some way, I feel depleted and drained. I then need a large dose of self-love and compassion to regain my emotional balance and refocus on what I need to do to get myself to a better place.

The power of developing self-worth through belief change was illustrated in my work with Gary, a man with a medical condition that caused him to suffer from severe muscle pain and chronic fatigue. Since Gary held a strong conviction that his worth depended on his ability to work and provide for his family, he felt inadequate, depressed and angry when his physical challenges forced him to leave the job he loved.

Over the course of our work together, Gary was able to understand that he was inherently worthy regardless of his abilities and began to feel good about the fact that he was an excellent father, a loving son and a sensitive and caring human being. His depression and anger consequently lifted and he felt much better about himself and his life.

Eventually, the choice of self-worth grows from a tiny shard of light piercing our self-imposed darkness to a radiant glow that spreads throughout our entire being, bathing us in happiness and peace. At a deep level, we realize that we - and everyone else in this world - deserve to experience this light. Through the compassion we increasingly extend to both ourselves and others, we begin to make this vision a reality.

Try These Strategies on for Size

➢ Recognize that any bad treatment you received from your parents or caretakers during your early years resulted from their own unhappiness, stress, etc. and was not a reflection of your worth in any way.

➢ Accept the love and support that others give as a gift to you and them.

➢ "Try on" the belief that you are inherently worthy regardless of how other people have treated you, your inability to live up to the expectations you or others have for yourself or the mistakes you have made.

➢ Understand that it is not selfish or narcissistic to feel worthy and that people who feel good about themselves are less self-absorbed and consequently better able to meet the needs of others.

➢ Forgive yourself for past mistakes so you can focus your energy on being the best person you can be rather than beating yourself up.

➢ Eliminate your need to judge other people or put them down because this undermines rather than enhances your self-worth, along with being unfair to them.

➢ Never compare yourself negatively to others.

Chapter 4

DO NOT PROJECT YOUR NEEDS ONTO OTHERS

We often make the mistake of projecting our needs onto others and feel angry, hurt, etc. when these people do not provide us what we're looking for. Although those who know us best can certainly meet some of our needs, it is impossible for anyone to know us well enough to consistently accomplish this complex task, and it would be unfair to expect that they do so even if they could. We alone know what we need and are generally much better able to provide it than anyone else.

In fact, one of the keys to a successful intimate relationship is for both partners to have realistic expectations for what they can expect from each other. Certainly, we have the right to receive emotional support when we are upset and encouragement to reach our goals. We also deserve to be treated with respect and never put down or shamed. Finally, we can expect that our partner will do what he or she can to help us grow into our best selves.

However, it is unreasonable and unrealistic to expect our partners to "make" us happy or somehow transform themselves into our ideal partner, which they are unlikely to be able to do even if they devoted their life to this lofty goal. In fact, the more we communicate to our partners that they fall short of our expectations, the less motivated they will probably be to make any changes in how they are or treat us.

Early on in my marriage, I made the mistake of assuming that it was Anita's responsibility to take away the hole I felt within. Not surprisingly, this expectation led to a great deal of conflict. Whenever I angrily pleaded with her to fill me up and make me happy, she wisely responded that I had to figure this out for myself because it was beyond her control. Although at first this seemed like an impossible task, I gradually began to focus on meeting my own needs, which led me to achieve a previously unknown level of emotional freedom.

My efforts included spending more time going by myself to the woods, sporting events, music concerts and the Jersey shore.

As I realized I had the capacity to meet my own needs, I released Anita from being responsible for my happiness, which significantly improved the quality of our relationship and enabled her to focus her energy on meeting her own needs instead of mine.

Over the years, I have worked with many clients who experience an even deeper hole within themselves because their needs were not adequately met during their childhoods. They spend their lives looking to their romantic partners, friends, parents or even children to fill this hole. When it doesn't get filled, they often blame others for being uncaring or insensitive. Sadly, their neediness often drives others away, leaving them even more empty and desperate.

Although I provide these clients with as much caring and support as I can, the most important thing I can do is help them understand that they will never find anyone who can fill them up with what they need. The reason is that no adult relationship can provide the devoted, consistent, multifaceted care that every child deserves to receive from unconditionally loving parents. After they finally let go of their fantasy that someone else can provide them with all they need, they can finally turn their attention to their *own* capacity to give themselves the attuned, loving care that they sorely lacked in childhood.

Clearly, one of the most self-compassionate and empowering things we can do is to let go of our projections onto others and take full responsibility for our happiness. Rather than wasting our energy trying to get other people to meet our needs, we can now invest it in our own self-care. Not only do we feel much better about ourselves and our lives, but our relationships improve because they are not impaired by our unrealistic expectations. Rather than view our connections to others as a means to an end, we can simply enjoy them.

<u>Try These Strategies on for Size</u>

➤ Do not project your needs onto others because you are likely to be left feeling hurt, angry, etc. when these people do not provide you with what you are looking for.
➤ Recognize that you know best what you need and are generally better able to provide it than others who have their own needs to look after.

> ➤ Develop realistic expectations in your intimate relationships and know that it is not your partner's responsibility to "make" you happy.
> ➤ Reinvest the energy you spend trying to get others to meet your needs into your own self-care.

Chapter 5

SANDY'S STORY

Sandy sought therapy with me after a lifetime of depression, low self-worth and relationship difficulties. She was highly aware that most of her emotional problems were caused by the fact that her mother had never acted in a loving manner towards her or provided her with the validation she craved. It was particularly painful for her to remember that as a young girl, she longed for her mother to give her the same attention she showered on her older brother, who could do nothing wrong in her mother's eyes.

Although Sandy had a close relationship with her father, who had tried hard to meet her emotional needs, she believed that there was something deeply wrong with her that caused her mother to treat her with such indifference. In an effort to perfect herself and therefore win her mother's love, she judged herself harshly from an early age. However, rather than help her feel more lovable, her relentless self-criticism drove her to increasingly deeper levels of depression, which she described as a black cloud hanging over her at all times.

Sandy sought to fill the deep emotional hole within by looking for others to give her the approval and attention she hadn't received from her mother. Sadly, her emotional neediness often drove people away, leaving her in even greater despair. In an effort to protect herself, Sandy retreated into her own shell, longing for connection with others, but too fearful to venture out of her self-imposed isolation.

Sandy did report that she had dated a few men who really cared about her. However, her sense of unworthiness made her feel undeserving of their love and it was safer for her to end these relationships than take the risks inherent in developing a closer emotional connection that she might eventually lose.

At the end of our first session, I emphatically told Sandy, "You are and have always been worthy and lovable. Your mother's bad treatment toward you resulted from her own emotional limitations and unhappiness and was in no way a reflection of who you are."

I will always remember her wide-eyed, tearful expression as she listened to my words. "I want to believe it," she whispered.

I also encouraged Sandy to talk to herself out loud like she was her own best friend as she drove home after our first session and continue to do so as often as possible until we met again. When she asked me how many positive things she should say to herself, I suggested that she start with a million (as I do with all of my clients who suffer from depression) and then evaluate how well this strategy was working. Sandy laughed in spite of herself.

Of course, no magical transformation occurred during Sandy's first session. But I knew from the hopeful look on her face that I had succeeded in creating a crack in her previously rock-solid belief that something was profoundly wrong with her. I wanted to expand this crack in any way possible until she replaced her erroneous and self-defeating sense of low self-worth with deep and abiding self-love. I also planned to guide her through the other portals to self-compassion described in this book.

Sandy began our following session by reporting that her depression was already beginning to lift. We then developed a "game plan" that outlined what else she could do to give herself the gifts of self-compassion and effective self-care. Her plan included being mindful of every time she made negative self-judgments and countering them with loving thoughts about herself. She also committed to "trying on" the belief that she was completely lovable and worthy, regardless of how her mother or others had treated her. Finally, she decided to engage more in activities she enjoyed, such as dancing and writing poetry.

Over the next several weeks, Sandy put our plan into practice and she began to feel much better about herself and her life. We then focused on how unrealistic it was for her to expect others to provide her with the love and support she had so painfully lacked during her formative years. She started to understand that adult relationships were unlikely to eliminate her sense of emptiness, and that she was in a much better position to do this herself because she alone knew what she wanted and needed at any moment.

Sandy was finally free to enjoy her interactions with others without the burden of her unrealizable expectations. Consequently, her relationships improved as she was able to relax and be her interesting and witty self. Rather than retreat into herself for self-protection, she began to expand her social horizons and reported that she felt excited about the relationship possibilities ahead of her.

Sandy also worked to eliminate her belief that she had to be perfect for others to like her. Even though she was very accepting of the faults of others, she had always assumed she could not have any herself or risk social rejection. I pointed out that we generally feel more connected to others when we share our mutual vulnerabilities and feel inadequate when in the presence of people we view as perfect. Although taken aback by the fact that she had lived her life under a false premise, she felt relieved to finally let go of her need to be perfect, which hurt rather than helped her relationships and was impossible to achieve.

The most challenging aspect of our work together was addressing Sandy's desire to come to some resolution in her relationship with her mother, who was divorced from her father and as emotionally distant as ever from Sandy. We agreed to begin this process through role-play, which I often use to help clients resolve difficult relationship issues. I played the part of Sandy's mother and Sandy began our interchange by saying with a great deal of emotion in her voice, "I have tried all my life to get you to love me, but you never once acted like you cared."

We subsequently went back and forth as she told me in many different ways how much I had hurt her and how much she wanted a closer relationship. In turn, I was highly defensive and repeatedly stated that I had done the best I could or acted callous to Sandy's pain. At the end of our very intense role-play, we were both emotionally drained.

Although Sandy had spent a great deal of psychic energy throughout her life having internal dialogues with her mother, she had never told her out loud how she felt about being treated so indifferently and it was highly cathartic for her even though it was just a role-play. However, Sandy believed that there was almost no chance that her mother would engage with her in the sort of dialogue we role-played, so she decided not to address her directly.

Sandy's ability to finally confront her mother through role-play and her realization that she was inherently worthy regardless of her mother's treatment lessened the power her mother held over her emotionally. In fact, Sandy reported that she actually felt sorry for her mother because she clearly did not have the capacity for caring relationships and probably suffered greatly in the midst of her emotional isolation. The lifelong, toxic spell that Sandy's relationship with her mother had cast over her was finally broken. She knew, at last, that she deserved to love herself and allow others to love her as well.

After 4 months of weekly sessions, Sandy had gained the self-compassion she needed to continue her path towards greater happiness and peace of mind without my guidance and we ended our work together. Rather than waking up each day with a sense of pervasive dread, she now experienced an excited anticipation about her future. The black cloud that had caused her despair was now gone, replaced with the glow of her new sense of worth and confidence in her ability to meet her own needs.

Chapter 6

GIVE YOURSELF THE GIFTS OF HAPPINESS AND PEACE OF MIND

Shortly after the birth of our daughter Nikki 27 years ago, it became evident that she was not developing typically. She made no eye contact, was very rigid in her body movements and often screamed nonstop for days at a time. Anita and I felt totally overwhelmed as we struggled to figure out how to meet her needs and overcome our feelings of parental inadequacy and uncertainty. We had no choice but to shut out the world around us and focus all of our energy on making it through each day as best we could.

Although we longed for a perspective that enabled us to celebrate rather than worry about Nikki's life, we were stuck in the despair we felt when she seemed beyond our reach and trapped in our fears that she would never be able to develop her abilities or live independently. Most importantly, we found ourselves in an unknown territory where our attitudes and beliefs had not adapted to the landscape.

When Nikki was almost 2-years-old, we attended a program at the Option Institute in Massachusetts, which helps children with special needs and their families. Shortly after we arrived, one of the program leaders asked us what we were afraid would happen if we let go of all of the unhappiness we were experiencing concerning Nikki's situation. I was puzzled by this question because it had never occurred to me that I had any option other than to be stressed out and anxious. I responded that maybe if I wasn't unhappy, I wouldn't be motivated to do everything I could to take good care of Nikki or people would think I was not concerned about her lack of development.

The leader then changed my life by asking a simple question, "Why don't you choose to be happy, regardless of the challenges you face with Nikki?" It was as if a door opened up in the maze of negative emotions we had been experiencing, allowing us to escape to a better place. In that moment, I realized that my unhappiness was not benefitting Nikki or anyone else.

I decided to take the risk of being happier and quickly realized that I did not need my unhappiness and stress to take effective care of Nikki. On the contrary, my increased happiness gave me a renewed sense of energy and possibility about my ability to make a difference in Nikki's life. I also finally recognized that I had the capacity to make each day a happy one, regardless of Nikki's level of development. In fact, when I returned home, my mother told me that I was a completely different person.

The staff at the Option Institute also taught us how to join Nikki in her world and stimulate her development through an intensive home-based treatment program that we eagerly began as soon as we arrived home. We worked with her many hours a day for the next couple of years to help her stand, make eye contact, pick up food and do many other new things. Eventually, she took her first step, which has been the most exciting event in my life.

Although Nikki has never learned to talk and continues to need a great deal of care, her relentless spirit and goodwill inspire me every day and I relish having her as a "soul mate." The privilege of being her father has taught me that a powerfully motivating and healing energy is created when I am able to provide her and everyone else in my life with unconditional acceptance. I have also learned to slow down and appreciate the importance of living in the present moment. Most importantly, I now know that my unhappiness doesn't benefit me, Nikki or anyone else, and I am much more effective when I give myself the gift of happiness.

This life-changing epiphany has compelled me to let go of the unhappiness I used to "give" myself because I mistakenly believed it would motivate me to make the changes I wanted to in my life. Clearly, there is nothing I can do better when I am unhappy than when I am happy. The knowledge that I can achieve happiness regardless of the challenges I face provides me with a deep sense of emotional freedom that I treasure.

In fact, whenever I feel unhappy I remind myself that this is my choice, rather than something beyond my control. Although this awareness does not usually give me instant happiness, my unhappiness is tempered and I make the conscious choice to do whatever I need to feel better such as talking to myself in a loving manner, taking better care of myself or finding solutions to whatever problems I am facing.

Why We Don't Choose Happiness

People often don't choose happiness because they believe they need their unhappiness to motivate them to overcome difficulties, become the person they want to be, etc. However, this is not the case. Unhappiness drains our spirit and impairs our ability to achieve our goals in contrast to happiness, which is energizing.

Although it is satisfying to complete a challenging task such as losing weight or finishing writing a book (I am not there yet), people who always look for something else to happen in their lives to "make" them happy usually only enjoy momentary satisfaction when they achieve one goal before they are unhappy they have not achieved another. They live their lives on an emotional roller coaster, always pushing the bar for happiness a bit higher. In fact, I fear that many people never reach this bar before taking their last breath and therefore never experience genuine fulfillment in their lives.

Even our nation's Founding Fathers thought we only had the right to the pursuit of happiness rather than happiness itself. However, at the risk of being a bit grandiose as well as over two-hundred years late, I declare that we have the right to be happy, with no limitations or conditions. In fact, this is one of the most important choices we can ever make because it has such a profound impact on the quality of our lives and our ability to be helpful to others.

I recently had a client inform me that she was "happy for no reason." When I inquired about how she achieved this highly desirable state of mind, she explained that she had always thought she needed to "earn" her happiness by being a good mother and having a successful career. However, as with all happy people, she finally realized she deserved the gift of happiness, regardless of how well her life was going.

If you are stuck on tying your happiness to your achievements, it's much better to shoot for an intrinsic goal such as being a more loving person, which you have a great deal of control over, rather than an extrinsic goal such as being the highest achiever in your field, which you have much less control over. In addition, goals that are driven by our ego such as the need to be the best at something generally separate us from others, whereas goals such as being kind and sensitive connect us to other people.

I remember my father telling me when I was a teenager that he would be happy when he had completed all the household tasks on his "to do" list. When I asked him why he couldn't be happy even as he was working towards his goals, he explained that he had to earn his happiness. Clearly, the concept of simply being happy without conditions was foreign to him and perhaps even threatening because it conflicted with one of his core beliefs.

However, during the last year of his life when he was in the late stages of Alzheimer's disease, I enjoyed a profound experience with my father when I took him for a drive just outside of the small town where I grew up. He spotted windmills on a distant hill and shouted, "Let's find them!" When we eventually wound up right underneath the windmills, he joyfully stared at them. Repeatedly, he exclaimed, "Wow!" I told him that I was enjoying being in this moment with him because he had spent so much of his life putting off his happiness. In a loving voice I will still remember even if I live a thousand years, he put his hand on my leg and said, "I like it too, son."

It is also difficult for people to give up their unhappiness because they believe it demonstrates that they are a caring person. For instance, a person might report that she or he is unhappy about children living in poverty. However, this is of no benefit to anyone, including the unfortunate children who would be better off if this person was completely happy, but sent them some food.

Finally, people sometimes choose to be unhappy in an attempt to control others. For instance, a wife might tell her husband that she is upset by his excessive drinking to motivate him to drink less. Although this type of emotional manipulation is common in most relationships and often works to some extent, it is not self-compassionate to base our level of happiness on someone else's behavior, over which we generally have limited, if any, control.

A more effective strategy is for this wife to instead maintain her happiness while she calmly informs her husband that she is concerned about his drinking because it is detrimental to his health and their marriage. She can also request that he stop drinking or alert him to what she intends to do if he does not change his drinking habits, such as leave the relationship. Regardless of whether or not this approach decreases his drinking, at least she is providing herself with excellent self-care by not giving up something as important as her happiness.

Let Go of Expectations

Our ability to choose happiness is largely contingent on our ability to let go of our expectations for how others should behave, how the events in our lives should unfold, etc. We are then free from the inevitable frustration we experience when these expectations are not met. We are also able to enjoy our life as it is rather than being frustrated that it doesn't measure up to some preconceived ideal. In fact, I have long observed that the happiest people I know expect the least and are consequently grateful for everything positive that comes their way, in contrast to people who expect the most and consequently suffer from a chronic sense of disappointment.

This doesn't mean that we shouldn't have a vision of who we want to be and what we want out of our lives. Indeed, a sense of direction in life gives us a good reason to get out of bed each morning and excitement about our future. However, when we believe that things should be a certain way for us to be happy, we set ourselves up for regret. The Chinese sage, Lao Tzu, summed it up well when he wrote, "Act without expectation."

Overcoming Trauma

I do not mean to suggest that it is possible to always be happy in life. Highly traumatic events almost always cause us to experience varying degrees of anxiety, sadness, despair, etc., which we initially have little or no control over. In fact, when I am working with a client who has recently experienced a traumatic event, it would be insensitive to suggest that he or she simply choose happiness while still in the midst of the grieving process. Instead, I listen to and join the client in his or her pain since trauma sticks to our soul until it is released through interactions with an attentive and caring human being.

I also encourage my clients to be self-compassionate by accepting their upset feelings rather than judging them, which only exacerbates their suffering. Clearly, there is no way we "should feel" following the death of a child or a sexual assault. In fact, our ability to still love ourselves regardless of what we are experiencing helps these feelings pass through us and dissipate rather than be blocked by our belief that we shouldn't be having them.

This was illustrated to me in my work with Lisa, who sought help due to the anguish and depression she was experiencing after her son's tragic death in a car crash. She had always viewed herself as a strong person who could overcome any challenge and frequently beat herself up for not being able to rid herself of her intense negative emotions. Rather than increase her pain through self-flagellation, I encouraged her to be self-compassionate by completely accepting everything she was feeling and bathing herself in self-love rather than criticism.

This was very difficult for Lisa because she had always judged herself harshly and put the needs of others ahead of her own. However, she realized that she had no choice but to focus on self-care because she had been emotionally deserted by her relatives, who told her in no uncertain terms she should "buck up" and "get over it." Although we had many sessions that left both of us in tears, the focus of our work gradually shifted to the important steps Lisa was taking on her journey to achieve self-compassion.

These steps included Lisa's new-found ability to recognize that she was still a strong person despite her painful emotions, talk to herself in a loving manner and develop strong emotional connections with people who supported rather than condemned her. She also took a trip by herself up a mountain where she performed a ritual that we had carefully planned, which enabled her to both celebrate and say goodbye to her son on a deeper level. It also provided her with an adventure to help her get "out of her head" and into the moment.

Although Lisa continued to feel the pain of her son's death, the intensity of her grief eventually diminished and she was able to experience moments of happiness and inner peace. For the first time in her life, she accepted herself as she was and became her own cheerleader rather than inner critic. It is ironic that the worst thing that ever happened to her also provided her with the stimulus she needed to rid herself of her inner demons and finally take great care of herself. In fact, she had no other choice if she was to climb out of her despair and heal her severe emotional wounds.

Lisa's experience is not unique. Life shattering events often give us a clearer view of what is most important in our lives and force us to find pathways to emotional healing in our efforts to recover from our unbearable pain. Although I certainly would not wish hard times on anyone, they can teach us valuable lessons, help us become more sensitive to the suffering of others and compel us to choose as much happiness and peace of mind as we can.

I learned that it is possible to move through the grief process following a trauma and still focus on choosing happiness after the death of my mother, who I will always treasure for the unconditional love she gave me throughout my life. In fact, she provided me with the approval I needed to accomplish this challenge.

During the last few years of her life, my mother often told me that she was worried about how I would cope with her death because we were extremely close. Each time, I responded by saying that it would be very hard, and then asking her if it would be okay for me to try to be happy even as I grappled with the pain of her death. She always responded emphatically that she always wanted me to be happy. Just before she died, I asked her one more time about this issue just to be sure. She responded, "Good Lord, son! Do we have to go through this again?"

Although I miss my mother every day, her permission to be happy despite my enormous loss has been her final gift to me and one that I long to thank her for in person. I often feel her presence and visualize that she is cheering me on in life and joyful that I have learned how to be self-compassionate. Rather than demonstrate my loyalty to her through unhappiness, I am honoring her wish for me to be happy to my benefit and the benefit of everyone around me.

Choose Peace of Mind Over Stress

Just as it is possible to choose happiness, we can also let go of stress and choose peace of mind, regardless of the challenges we face. An important component of this process is to recognize that *we generally cause our own stress* rather than outside events. For instance, traffic jams do not cause stress. If they did, everyone around us in this situation would experience stress. Although many people brim with impatience or anger, others sit patiently and peacefully, knowing that they have no control over the situation - only their reaction to it.

Many people have difficulty choosing peace of mind over stress because they believe that their stress helps them live their lives more effectively. In fact, stress depletes our energy and does not help us except in highly dangerous situations, when our limbic systems are automatically aroused to help us protect ourselves.

I learned this experientially many years ago when I used to feel a high level of stress before I conducted training for large groups of people. My queasy stomach and intense anxiety made it difficult for me to sleep the night before and the sleep I did achieve was often filled with dreams of public humiliation. After years of self-imposed and unnecessary suffering, I finally decided to take the risk of letting go of my stress. I quickly realized that I did not need stress to carefully prepare for and conduct my trainings. In fact, I was much more effective when I was relaxed and peaceful.

I encourage my clients to take the risk of letting go of stress to prove to themselves that it does not serve them in any way. I assure them that if their inner peace leads them to stay in bed all day and ignore their responsibilities, they can always return to being stressed. However, this never happens. On the contrary, clients who choose peace of mind always report that they accomplish more, are better at finding effective solutions to difficult problems and simply feel better.

People also have difficulty letting go of stress because they believe it is a badge of honor in our fast-paced society, proving to themselves and others that they are responsible and hardworking. They often relish telling others about how stressed out they feel and view peaceful people with suspicion because they are clearly not "in the game."

However, being stressed out does not prove we are worthy or competent. It only reduces our quality of life and significantly increases the chances that we will suffer from high blood pressure, heart disease and other serious health problems. It also puts us at risk for addictions, which temporarily dull our emotional pain. Finally, it takes a huge toll on our relationships, because most people eventually get tired of hearing about our stress when they have their own challenges to overcome.

Try These Strategies on for Size

> ➤ Recognize that we "give" ourselves unhappiness because we mistakenly believe that we need it to make changes in our lives.
> ➤ Choose as much happiness and peace of mind as you can at any given moment.
> ➤ Understand that you do not need to be unhappy to prove that you are a caring person.
> ➤ Do not use your unhappiness to control others. Instead, maintain your happiness even as you assert your needs or make requests of others.
> ➤ Know that happiness is your inherent right rather than something you have to earn.
> ➤ When you are experiencing intense emotions following a traumatic event, accept all of your feelings rather than judging them and focus on being highly self-compassionate.
> ➤ Let go of all of your expectations for life so you can enjoy it as it is rather than compare it to some preconceived ideal, which leads to disappointment.
> ➤ Understand that stress drains your energy and serves no purpose outside of highly dangerous situations.
> ➤ Recognize that it is generally a waste of energy to tell others how stressed out you are because they have their own challenges to grapple with.

Chapter 7

TAKE GREAT CARE OF YOURSELF

One of the most self-compassionate things we can do is to take great care of our emotional, physical and social needs. In fact, each day presents us with countless choices about how to spend our time and focus our energies. When we respond to these opportunities in ways that bring us meaning, pleasure, comfort, inner peace and good health, we feel satisfied with our lives. When we ignore our needs, we feel frustrated and depleted.

The key to following our bliss is to prioritize our needs and manage our time effectively so that we can meet them. In fact, the happiest people I know maintain a laser-like focus on doing whatever is most fulfilling to them, whether this involves walking in the woods, playing the flute or simply drinking hot cider in front of a roaring fire. They do not waste their time on activities that add nothing to their lives, drain their spirit or impair their health.

For many of us, the challenge is to find the time to take effective care of ourselves given our work and family responsibilities. This was painfully true for me early on in Nikki's life, when Anita and I struggled to meet her needs and find professionals who could help her. I learned that the only way I could avoid burnout - which always seemed to be lurking just around the corner - was to improve my self-care. I began meditating each day to find a place of peace that transcended the external pressures I faced, cut back on my work hours to free up more time to focus on the home front and began seeing a therapist for support and guidance.

In fact, if I hadn't figured out how to take better care of myself, I would have found it much more difficult to provide Nikki with the daily care she has always needed, which includes dressing, feeding and bathing as well as changing her pull-ups and keeping an eye on her to make sure she is safe. Fortunately, Anita is an equal partner in this endeavor and our ability to work together as a team has helped us to take good care of Nikki and solidify our marriage.

My motivation to take great care of myself intensified a few years ago. After foolishly ignoring chest pains for three weeks, I finally went to a cardiologist who looked at my EKG results, informed me that I may have had a heart attack and called an ambulance. An hour later, I received a stent, which opened up an artery that had been 99 percent blocked. Two doctors subsequently told me that I was lucky to be alive.

I arrived home a few days later with a burning desire to reduce the panic I felt about my future and regain a sense of control over my life. In order to lower my high cholesterol and improve my heart health, I started following a plant-based diet and exercising on a daily basis. After four months of eating just salads, fruits, beans and nuts, I lost 40 pounds and cut my total cholesterol level in half.

I have maintained my healthy eating habits ever since and avoid the foods that probably contributed to my medical crisis, such as meat, dairy products, oils and snack foods. Not only have I significantly reduced my chances of heart trouble, but I have regained a sense of confidence in my future. In fact, my decision to eat more healthy food is one of the most self-compassionate things I have ever done for myself.

People sometimes ask how I can live without eating ice cream, french fries, potato chips or the many other foods that taste great, but put us at risk for serious health problems. I respond that it is not difficult at all given my goal of living a vital life into a second century. I love my life and am almost obsessed (actually, totally obsessed if you ask Anita) with my commitment to not do anything that might contribute to it ending.

Spend Time Alone

Another way I take great care of myself is by spending time alone so I can replenish myself by focusing solely on meeting my own needs. It took me a long time to learn how to relish solitude because I am by nature a highly social person and love to connect on some level with almost everyone I come into contact with. In fact, one of my favorite things to do is engage in meaningful conversations with others, even total strangers. I used to feel restless and empty whenever I was by myself because most of my identity was based on my relationships.

However, as I learned to treat myself with compassion and be my own best friend, I began to crave time alone. The ideal place for me to savor solitude is at our family cabin where I am free to do exactly what I need to do to experience a sense of rejuvenation and peace. My perfect days include canoeing on the Rancocas cedar stream, reading, playing my guitar, running, basking in the natural beauty all around me and, best of all, listening to the whippoorwills sing their soft notes over the pines as the evening sets in. In fact, I am currently in the middle of one of these perfect days at this cabin as I write these words.

I have come to realize that I do not need to be at the cabin to live my ideal life. In fact, I often sit in my home office first thing in the morning and carefully choose the ingredients I want to put into every day. On days that are filled with responsibilities, I think through how I can be at the top of my game and what I am going to do at the end of the day to reward myself.

When I have more free time, I plan out how I can achieve an effective balance between getting things done and finding happiness and meaning through fulfilling activities. I also focus on the other areas of my life that are important to me, such as spending quality time with my family and maintaining strong connections with my siblings, extended family and close friends.

Effective Self-Care is Not Selfish

People are often afraid to take great care of themselves because they mistakenly believe that it is "selfish" to meet their own needs. Certainly, it is selfish to look out for oneself at the expense of others. However, there is nothing selfish about effective self-care. The challenge is to figure out how we can accomplish this important task without being unfair to others.

I search for this balance by going within myself and taking a hard look at the impact of my choices. I am usually surprised at how quickly I am able to decide if my efforts to take care of myself negatively impact anyone else. I highly value my inner barometer concerning how I can balance my needs with the needs of others and have developed faith in what it tells me. Fortunately, I never have to question the fairness of giving myself the gifts of inner peace and happiness, because they exist in abundance and are available to everyone.

Hopefully, we are all aware that treating others badly is wrong and can cause great pain. Not only is it compassionate to respect the rights of others, but self-compassionate as well. We all have to live within ourselves, and most of us suffer when we treat others poorly. In fact, it is impossible to feel good about ourselves (unless we are sociopaths) if we consistently behave in ways that we know are unfair.

Although many men have difficulty taking good care of themselves, I believe that effective self-care is even more challenging for women, who are often socialized to put their needs aside in favor of taking care of others. The difficulty women have in prioritizing themselves likely stems from the fact that they have historically shouldered the responsibility for taking care of their children, who may suffer if their mothers are too focused on their own needs.

Just imagine that 40,000 years ago a mother leaves her young children in their cave to take a dip in the river on a hot summer day. Upon returning, she finds that one of them has fallen and been seriously injured. She experiences deep guilt and is shamed by the other members of her tribe, hard wiring into the memory center of her brain the importance of putting her needs aside for the benefit of her children. This memory and other similar ones are passed down through female genes over hundreds of generations, resulting in modern day women often feeling guilty whenever they focus on meeting their own needs.

Listen to Yourself

One of the most rewarding aspects of my work with clients is supporting them in the process of learning how to take great care of themselves. After their self-care program begins to develop momentum, they often do not need any more help from me. Sometimes they even call me years later to tell me how they have benefited from their self-care and compassion.

I start by asking clients to identify everything they do that brings them happiness, pleasure, inner peace and good health. I then encourage them to commit to finding more daily time to do these things. Although this may appear to be easy, many people find it challenging because they simply are not used to meeting their own needs.

This is usually because we take our cues for how to live our lives from the messages we receive from significant others rather than ourselves. If we grew up with the belief that we should meet our parents' needs and/or were shamed every time we did something for ourselves, we instinctively focus on the needs of others and assess our worth based on how effectively we are able to be of service to them. We consequently lose our ability to listen and respond to the inner voice that only we can hear - the voice that tells us what we need to do at any given moment to take great care of ourselves.

A new world of possibilities opens up for my clients after they have cleared out all the erroneous beliefs that prevent them from listening to their inner voice. They are able to find a healthier balance between meeting their own needs and attending to the needs of others. Paradoxically, this process often improves rather than impairs their relationships because they feel better about themselves and are able to set healthier boundaries. Consequently, they do not experience the underlying resentment that builds up when they allow others to take advantage of them.

Eliminate Unhealthy Behaviors

A second way I empower my clients to take better care of themselves is to teach them strategies to eliminate self-destructive behaviors. This is challenging because people in emotional pain understandably self-medicate through behaviors such as drinking too much alcohol, abusing drugs or overeating. Although all of these behaviors bring temporary relief, they eventually damage one's health, relationships and even the ability to function effectively.

I have found that one of the best ways to help clients make the choice not to engage in self-destructive behaviors is to help them change what they are thinking just before they reach for their third glass of wine or bowl of ice cream. For instance, rather than focus on how much comfort and pleasure they will experience by consuming the substance at hand, they can turn their thoughts to the longer-term consequences of their actions, including the fact that they are likely to feel even worse when the "high" they are seeking dissipates. I also encourage them to focus on positive outcomes, such as how good they will feel about themselves if they make a healthier choice.

Practice Forgiveness

A third way I help my clients take care of themselves is by encouraging them to forgive themselves for anything they have done that has been destructive to themselves or others. This does not absolve them of the responsibility of making amends for their mistakes. It simply means that they let go of negative feelings such as guilt, shame or regret, which drain their energy and often lead them to be more self-absorbed.

Many of us believe that guilt and shame motivate us to do the right thing. However, it is not necessary to experience these emotions to live highly moral lives. We can achieve these important goals by simply growing into our best selves and being fair and sensitive to our fellow human beings. In fact, the most giving people I know quickly forgive themselves for their mistakes rather than wallowing in guilt so they can focus their energy on being of service to others.

My work with Joe illustrates this point. He had made some poor decisions that were hurtful to his wife and left him drowning in guilt and shame. Although Joe had initially done an effective job of taking full responsibility for his mistakes, whenever his wife subsequently brought them up, he protected himself by withdrawing from her emotionally or lashing out at her in anger, which only left her feeling more hurt and distant.

I pointed out to him that his guilt and shame were not serving him or his marriage well. I encouraged him to make amends to his wife by letting these feelings go, listening attentively to her feelings and focusing on meeting her needs rather than his. Although difficult, he was able to achieve these goals, which ended their downward marital spiral and enabled him and his wife to regain their sense of mutual trust and emotional connection.

It is also self-compassionate to forgive others for the ways in which they have hurt us rather than hold onto negative emotions such as anger, which impair our happiness and peace of mind. Indeed, we forgive for ourselves rather than for those who have hurt us. This neither means that we forget the painful things that we have experienced, nor that we're powerless. We can forgive others and still hold them accountable for what they have done to us, let them know what we expect them to do to make amends and effectively protect ourselves from being hurt in the future.

Address Mistreatment

A final way I assist my clients in taking better care of themselves is to help them effectively address those who have mistreated them. This is often difficult for people who were neglected or abused during their childhoods because they often believe that they somehow deserved the bad treatment they received and/or do not have the gumption they need to stand up for themselves. Unfortunately, their willingness to put up with unfair treatment leads the perpetrator to believe that his or her behavior is acceptable, which often fuels further mistreatment.

However, as clients begin to feel more worthy during the course of our work together, they recognize that they deserve to always be treated with sensitivity and respect. We then discuss strategies they can use to effectively address people who are mistreating them and practice these strategies through role-play. I have found that one of the most effective strategies is to use "meta-communication" questions such as, "What gives you the right to treat me the way you do?" or "What is it about me, you or how you view the world that would possibly lead you to think that the way you are treating me is fair?"

These questions are designed to catch people off guard and force them to assess the impact of their behavior. If the perpetrator responds that his or her behavior is not unfair, it simply leads to another question such as, "Why do you think you are in a better position to assess the fairness of your behavior, when I am the one who is being hurt by it?" The beauty of these types of questions is that they enable us to avoid point-counterpoint arguments and gain a greater sense of empowerment in difficult relationships.

Another useful strategy is to specify exactly what changes the person needs to make to continue the relationship. For example, you might say, "I can't make you stop yelling at me, but if you continue, I will have no choice but to sever our connection." This strategy puts the burden of change directly on the perpetrator and often compels him or her to behave more appropriately.

Of course, we can't use this kind of strategy with children who need our care. However, it is still possible to set clear limits to take care of ourselves. For instance, my son, Darqui, went through a period when he was 12 years old where he used a lot of offensive language. Consequences such as taking something away from him when he behaved badly had never worked, so the only way I could protect myself was to inform him that I needed to distance myself from him a bit when he used offensive language.

I did not stop loving Darqui or meeting his needs. I just changed the only thing I had any power over in the situation, which was my own behavior. Over time, Darqui almost completely eliminated his use of offensive language. I am not clear if my behavior caused this change, but it certainly respected his freedom, dramatically reduced the tension between us and enabled me to take better care of myself.

Eliminate Toxic Relationships

Unfortunately, meta-communication questions and viable limit-setting do not always stop other people from mistreating us. When this is the case, we have no other choice but to end the relationship if we are committed to taking great care of ourselves. Although this is often a painful process, it is a cornerstone of self-compassion and eventually enables us to experience increased levels of self-worth, happiness and inner peace.

Many years ago, I worked with Julie, a woman who sought marital therapy to improve her relationship with a man who routinely spoke to her in demeaning ways and occasionally physically abused her. Although she hated the way Carl treated her, Julie was terrified by his repeated threat that he was going to leave her and would cling to his leg to prevent him from walking out the door. Our joint sessions dissolved into shouting matches between Julie and Carl, which led me to work with them each individually.

Julie spent many sessions describing her childhood during which her father regularly told her that she would never amount to anything and physically abused her. Although she hated her father and had broken off contact with him, all of her romantic relationships had been with abusive men. She was able to recognize that she was trying to prove to herself that she was lovable by choosing men like her father and then trying to win the love from them that she had never received as a child.

Over the course of our work together, Julie eventually understood that she was worthy and lovable regardless of how her father had treated her and decided that she needed to end her marriage if she was to live a healthy life. However, her terror of being alone prevented her from doing so.

Our work together took a crucial turn when Julie informed me that she frequently dreamed that she was inside a bird's egg that was sitting alone in a nest. She readily agreed with my assessment that this dream represented her strong desire for someone to take care of her. Rather than stay within the limits of her shell forever, she took me up on my suggestion that she pretend she was this bird's mother and begin to take better care of herself by giving herself the love, comfort and safety she had always craved.

Julie's realization that she could take effective care of herself gave her the confidence and empowerment she needed to grow her wings and leave the nest. Now that she knew her needs would always be met, she no longer feared living alone. She packed up, changed her phone number and moved into a new living situation that her husband knew nothing about. Many years after our work ended, she called to let me know she was happier than she had ever been in her life and no longer had any attraction to men like her father.

My life has been enriched by the many ways my clients have learned to take great care of themselves and I often marvel at the courage and tenacity they exhibit during this process. They finally feel whole inside and free from their dependency on others because they are now able to meet their own needs.

I hope you too are able to enjoy the rich rewards of effective self-care by following your inner voice that always knows what you need to do at any given moment to live the life you want.

<u>Try These Strategies on for Size</u>

➢ Follow your bliss by prioritizing your needs and managing your time so these needs can be met.

➢ Learn how to relish solitude where you are free to focus on meeting your own needs rather than the needs of others.

➢ Plan and live out "perfect days" that bring you meaning, happiness, pleasure, inner peace and great health.

➢ Know that it is not selfish to take great care of yourself as long as you are not unfair to other people in the process.

➢ Listen and respond to your "inner voice" that tells you what you need to do at any given moment to meet your needs.

➢ Eliminate unhealthy behaviors.

➢ Recognize that you do not need to experience guilt or shame to live a moral life or be the best person you can be.

➢ Understand that you never deserve mistreatment and protect yourself by asking questions that force others to assess their unfair behavior, setting viable limits and severing toxic relationships.

Chapter 8

"TUNE INTO" YOUR AUTHENTIC SELF

As long as we are conscious, it is difficult to not focus on our thoughts. If they help us to function more effectively or solve problems, there is no reason not to. However, many people go around and around in their heads with endless cycles of analysis, worry and rumination that are exhausting and serve no cogent purpose. Buddhists refer to this mental distraction as the "monkeys in the trees" and a client recently described it more simply as, "The nonsense in our heads."

When I am working with clients who have a hard time getting "out of their heads," I help them recognize that there is a part of them that exists beyond their thoughts by asking them to think about one thing and then switch their focus to something else. I then ask them who is doing the switching and respond to their look of puzzlement by explaining that we all have an integral part of ourselves that transcends our thoughts and has the capacity to observe or change them. I go on to explain that if we were simply our thoughts, we would have no control over them.

I then teach them a number of portals they can use to reduce or eliminate their attachment to their thoughts and "tune into" this deeper, more authentic part of themselves. One portal is for them to recognize that their thoughts are always changing, just like clouds passing through the sky. Therefore, if they allow their thoughts to define who they are, this definition will be outdated in the next instant.

Another portal is for my clients to understand that just because they think something, it doesn't make it true. Thoughts are constructions that originate within us and may or may not have any connection to reality. An example of this truth comes at the end of the movie, *A Beautiful Mind*, when Russell Crowe, who plays Princeton professor John Nash, firmly tells the fictional characters who have haunted him throughout his adult life that he is not going to pay them any more attention.

Of course, the challenge is to "tune into" our thoughts when they are serving us well and "tune them out" when they aren't. A good way to measure this is to gauge whether they lead us to live more effective lives or just take up psychic energy without reaping any results. Clearly, we only go around and around in our heads when we are unable to solve a challenging problem. If we could solve it, we would.

After my clients have determined that certain thoughts are not helping them, they need to stop focusing on them even if they can't make them go away entirely. One useful strategy is for them to imagine that all of the components of their psyche make up their inner house. They need to leave the room containing the thoughts that are troubling them, lock the door and enter a room that brings them greater happiness and inner peace.

Secondly, I suggest that my clients visualize that the negative inner scripts they play out in their heads are like a movie they are watching in a theater and that they have the power to change these scripts in any way they want. For instance, when they are ruminating about a past painful experience, they can replace it with a positive memory or something they are looking forward to doing. They can also turn off the movie and enter a more peaceful place within themselves.

Finally, I encourage my clients to picture that their unwanted thoughts are knocking at their front door. Rather than opening the door and allowing them in, they need to firmly tell their thoughts, "Go away and don't bother me again!" Just like an unwelcome neighbor, their thoughts eventually get tired of being thwarted and give up trying to invade their psyche.

When my clients are unable to let go of specific ruminations, I encourage them to give themselves a finite period of time to dwell on them before they change their focus. For instance, they could decide to obsess about how much they hate their job until they arrive home after work and then put all their energy into playing with their children or making dinner. In fact, a cousin of mine hung a proclamation over her front door which prevented any negative thoughts from entering her house along with her.

As my clients develop their ability to detach from their thoughts, they focus less on their problems, which reduces their identification with them. Consequently, they are able to put some space around their problems and view them from a more detached perspective. As they recognize that their problems do not define who they are, their spirits lift and they have more energy to explore other parts of themselves or simply enjoy the present moment.

Enter Your Authentic Self

Where can we go to escape our unwanted thoughts and experience a sense of who we really are? This question has been answered by therapists, writers, theologians, philosophers, poets, musicians and countless others over the centuries. In different ways, all of them have described a place within we can all access that transcends our thoughts and problems.

I view this place as our authentic self. It is an inner realm we can go to any time we choose to experience a sense of peace and presence amidst the noise within our own heads and the world around us. It is a permanent part of us that does not change as we experience life's challenges, develop different outward identities or go through the aging process. In a nutshell, it is who we are at our most basic level.

One way to access your authentic self is to visualize that you're on a raft on the surface of the ocean. You are happy when the sun is shining and you are surrounded by dolphins, and you're upset when you are tossed about by the waves or out of food. Now imagine that you are diving deep underneath the ocean surface to the inner sanctuary of your authentic self that protects you from the ups and downs of the outside world. When you arrive, you are likely to feel that you have come back home to a place that part of you has never left.

Another is to think back to your childhood and connect with the essential part of yourself that has never changed even as your life experiences have. This process is often enhanced when you look intently at old pictures of yourself or read things you wrote many years ago. Clearly, this durable component of your psyche exists beyond your ever-changing thoughts, feelings and perceptions.

During my mother's final year of life, she often commented that she felt like she was still age 10, sitting on her favorite rock outside her house in White Marsh, Pennsylvania and imagining fairies playing all around her. This was not simply a happy memory, but a significant, playful part of her authentic self that was as alive and vital as it had been 75 years earlier. Even in the midst of her significant medical challenges, her undaunted spirit still glowed with the same light it always had.

In a similar vein, I recently saw a picture of myself when I was about 11 years old that my sister posted on Facebook. I stared at myself for a long time and connected with an inner "Nateness" that was as unique and innate (pun intended) within me then as it is now. Even after 61 years of life's ups and downs, I felt a deep connection with my true self that will continue to define and anchor my existence until my last breath and maybe even beyond - a concept that is outside the domain of this book.

Some people don't experience their authentic selves until just before they die, when their transient identities have been stripped away. They finally enter their authentic selves and often illustrate this through their profound sense of peace and joy that comes as a surprise to grieving family members. A key motivation in writing this book is to help you find this place well before the last moments of your life.

Stay In Your Authentic Self

When I first began to "tune into" my authentic, inner self, I went there only when I needed some respite from the turmoil of the outside world, like a quick trip to a warm vacation spot. However, one of the most compelling discoveries I have made is that I can stay in this peaceful place almost all of the time and still live an effective life in the outside world. Rather than cause me to forget my responsibilities, I am much better able to focus clearly on what I need to do at any given moment, free from stress and the distraction of unwanted thoughts.

I am also much less reactive to external events when I am in the friendly confines of my authentic self. For instance, I recently got stuck in a traffic jam while on my way to teach my classes at Temple University. Rather than get caught up in my fears of being late, I took the opportunity to journey deep inside of myself and felt a remarkable sense of calm and peace, even amidst the stressed out people around me honking their horns and jockeying to get into a better lane. I felt joyful to be alive and profoundly aware that the essence of my life existed in a transcendent place deep within me that was not affected in any way by my arrival time or any other event in the outside world. When I did arrive (just in the nick of time), I was relaxed and in an excellent frame of mind to teach my classes.

I am highly aware when I am in the realm of thought and when I am in my authentic self, and each of these states of being is uniquely different. When I am focused on my thoughts, I can actually feel them flowing through the top of my head, like electricity surging through a maze of different wires. In contrast, my authentic self feels grounded and secure, like a sturdy lighthouse that helps me find my way in all kinds of weather. I can choose to be in my thoughts or my authentic self like changing the dial on an old-fashioned radio, depending on what aspect of my psyche I want to experience.

Whenever I am unable to solve a challenging problem through rational thought, I put it in an internal box I call my "hopper" and stop thinking about it rather than wasting my energy repeatedly running into the same brick wall. Inevitably, and often when I least expect it, a solution mysteriously appears from my wise, authentic self. I have come to call this process a "knowing," because the answers I am seeking seem to have been within me all along, just waiting to be stumbled upon as soon as I stop looking for them.

Many of my clients find it helpful to learn how to identify and counter the irrational thoughts that are causing their unhappiness through what is commonly known as positive self-talk. However, I have found that this strategy generally is not as helpful as entering their authentic selves because it often creates an internal debate that limits their ability to simply enjoy the present moment. In addition, many clients report that their unwanted thoughts are too powerful to counter and actually become stronger when challenged. In contrast, these thoughts fade away along with their unhappiness when they are able to get "out of their heads" and find a place of peace within.

I encourage all of my clients to journey into the serenity of their authentic selves, regardless of the severity of their challenges. For instance, a number of years ago, I made a home visit to see Jack, a young man who suffered from such severe multiple sclerosis that he could not voluntarily move any part of his body other than his face. It took a great deal of energy for him to speak and it was difficult to hear him over the sounds of the machines he was hooked up to that kept him alive.

However, Jack was able to verbalize his many frustrations, which included his lack of mobility, his concern that his mother was "burned out" by all of the care he needed and the acute stress of his frequent hospitalizations. Although I felt a profound sense of sadness about Jack's dire situation, I also knew that I could not be a resource to him if I simply joined him in his despair. Consequently, I encouraged him to "tune into" a deeper place within him that transcended his physical limitations and emotional pain.

Jack was initially confused by this question as most of my clients are. However, he was intrigued by the possibility that he might be able to experience a previously unknown sense of inner peace. I gave him a few minutes to access his authentic self through visualization and knew that he had succeeded when he began to smile for the first time since we began our session. His spirits continued to lift as we discussed the fact that he always had the freedom to enter this inner realm, which was not impacted in any way by his medical problems.

I am painfully aware that my work with Jack did not end his suffering. However, I am honored that I was able to help him enter into his authentic self and experience at least some inner peace amidst all he was grappling with.

I hope that you too are able to enter your authentic self and spend as much time there as you can. You will finally be free to experience the joys of happiness and peace of mind, regardless of the difficulties you face in the outside world.

Try These Strategies on for Size

- ➢ Reduce or eliminate your attachment to your unwanted thoughts by recognizing that they are always changing and do not define your identity.
- ➢ Develop the ability to "tune into" your authentic self, which is a permanent and deeper part of yourself that transcends your thoughts and feelings.
- ➢ Access your authentic self by looking at pictures from your childhood and connecting with the part of you that never changes.

> ➢ Become aware of when you are focused on your thoughts and when you are in the realm of your authentic self and develop the ability to select which aspect of your psyche you want to be in at any given moment.
> ➢ Recognize that you can remain in your authentic self and still lead an effective life in the outside world.
> ➢ When you are unable to solve a challenging problem through rational thought, let it go and trust that a solution will come to you when you least expect it.

Chapter 9
ELIMINATE NEGATIVE REACTIONS

One of the most self-compassionate things we can do is to train ourselves to respond to challenging life situations in a calm and focused manner rather than with anger, frustration or other negative emotions. Although responding to difficulties with equanimity is no easy matter, it is a major portal into the land of inner peace and happiness.

A profound example of our ability to choose our reaction to difficult circumstances is described in Viktor Frankl's book, *Man's Search for Meaning.* While imprisoned in a Nazi concentration camp during World War II, Frankl realized that the only thing his captors could not take away from him was his ability to choose his reaction to the brutal treatment and severe deprivation he and his fellow inmates were subjected to on a daily basis. Rather than slip into the hopelessness that drove many around him to throw themselves into the electric fences that held them captive, Frankl decided to find meaning in his experience and do everything he could to minister to the emotional needs of his fellow prisoners.

Whenever I feel overwhelmed by my life circumstances, I think about Frankl's ability to maintain his emotional balance amidst the horror he faced and live as constructive a life as possible. I figure that if he could choose his response to his dire situation, I can do the same with the far less serious challenges I face.

The first step in the process of eliminating our negative reactions is to make a deep commitment to ourselves that we are no longer going to react in a negative manner to anything that happens outside of us. We then need to practice stopping our emotional reactions before they engulf us. Key to this process is recognizing the visceral, physiological sensations we experience just before we have a negative emotional response, such as our muscles tightening or "seeing red." At that moment, we need to tell ourselves in no uncertain terms that we have the choice not to act on these sensations, regardless of how difficult this is.

In fact, whenever I begin to experience reactive anger or frustration, I visualize a steel garage door slamming down and severing the connection between whatever is happening around me and my emotional response to it. I am therefore free to choose my reaction to the situation I am facing, which leaves me with a solid sense of self-control and enables me to maintain my peace of mind in moments where I used to lose it. I also am free from having to repair the relational damage I caused by my angry outbursts and overcome the subsequent shame I experienced.

We can also give our negative emotions a name and view them as an external force trying to invade our psyche and rob us of our peace of mind. For instance, I recently worked with a 9-year-old boy who would go into frequent rages when he wasn't able to get his way and yell disrespectful things at his mother. I asked him to give his emotional outbursts a name and he decided on "angry man." I then told him to view "angry man" as an outside attacker, just like the zombies he shot at in the video games he loved to play. Finally, we brainstormed strategies he could use to keep "angry man" at bay, such as giving his mom a hug instead of being mean to her, telling himself he had a choice about how he reacted to frustration or engaging in relaxing activities such as lying on his bed and listening to music.

Going to the Balcony

The process of detaching from our negative emotional reactions is often referred to as "going to the balcony." While there, we can calmly and rationally review our options in the situation we face and decide the best course of action. Even a few seconds on the balcony buys us time to choose how we want to respond and helps prevent us from doing or saying something that escalates the situation or that we may later regret.

Most of my clients have never heard about the wonders of the balcony so I encourage them to imagine that they are caught up in some intense drama on a stage. Rather than reacting emotionally to this situation, I suggest that they visualize leaving the stage and going up to a balcony where they can look down on their drama from a more detached perspective, which I refer to as the "long view." When they are no longer in a reactive place, they can return to the stage with a clear plan about how to resolve the situation at hand, choose to leave the theater or simply stay on the balcony until they decide what to do. In any case, they are in control of themselves even if they are not able to control what is going on around them.

One of the most effective ways my clients are able to get to their balcony is through the visualizations I teach them to use, such as the steel door concept. Another one of my favorites is to encourage them to imagine that they are standing next to a gushing river of negative emotion whenever they begin to experience frustration, anger or other upset feelings. Rather than jumping into this river and becoming emotionally flooded, I suggest that they envision that they are turning away from the river and walking into a beautiful meadow. The farther away they go, the less chance there is that they will wind up in the river and be swept away by their escalating emotions.

I also encourage my clients to come up with their own visualizations because they know best what will work for them. For instance, I recently counseled a man who had lost his temper with his son and yelled something at him that he quickly regretted. When I asked him what he could think about to quell his anger, he immediately replied with the name of a professional hockey player he had recently observed just before a fight. He reported that this player was so angry that his face was beet red and the veins in his neck were bulging out. He remembered thinking that he never wanted to look this out of control and committed to saying this player's name repeatedly to himself every time anger began to spark up within him.

I often work with clients who have been referred to me due to serious problems with anger management. They generally begin therapy by describing the people or events that have "made" them mad. After I listen supportively to their stories, I help them understand that nothing can "make" them mad except themselves and that they always have options, regardless of the situation they face.

I also explain that people do not get rid of anger by expressing it. In fact, neurologists have discovered that the part of our brain that experiences anger thickens every time we get angry, just as our muscles gain strength when we do push-ups. In contrast, when we respond to challenging situations calmly, our brain biochemistry changes in ways that make it easier for us to do so again in the future.

Finally, I encourage my clients to identify a visualization they can use in the upcoming week to eliminate their angry reactions, regardless of the difficulties they face. They then practice this visualization as we role-play situations that have set their anger off until they have developed confidence in their self-control.

Although the use of visualizations may sound like a simplistic solution for clients who are chronically angry, I am often surprised to see how well they work, especially when clients are highly motivated to change. For instance, I worked with Eric, a teenage boy whose temper was so violent that he had to be accompanied by an adult at all times in school. In addition, he was forbidden to spend any unsupervised time with his girlfriend, who was on the verge of breaking up with him due to his frequent rages.

During our initial session, I told Eric about my own past difficulties controlling my temper and the steel garage door visualization that had changed my life, which he agreed to try. Finally, we discussed all of the ways he could benefit from controlling his temper, such as not losing his girlfriend, gaining more freedom in school and feeling in greater control of himself and his life.

Eric began our second session by telling me that the garage door concept had worked so well for him that he had gone an entire week without losing his temper. His girlfriend's mother, who had brought him to therapy, informed him that he was doing "awesome" and that she was very proud of him. We spent the remainder of the session role-playing how he could respond directly but calmly to challenging situations, such as another boy whistling at his girlfriend in the hall at his school.

Another example of how visualization helped one of my clients change his unwanted emotional reactions involved a 10-year-old boy who was brought to therapy by his mother because he was getting bullied in tee ball. Whenever Justin missed the ball, the other boys would make fun of him, causing him to burst into tears and experience humiliation.

When I asked him to name his favorite place, Justin responded that it was on the beach in Ocean City, New Jersey. I then asked him to close his eyes and visualize that he was sitting peacefully on this beach, enjoying the sound of the ocean waves and the feeling of the hot sun on his skin. After practicing this visualization a number of times, I encouraged Justin to go to Ocean City in his head the next time he missed the ball.

During our next session, Justin reported that the bullying had ended once he responded calmly, rather than tearfully, whenever he missed the ball. A few years later, I ran into him and his mother at our local supermarket. He looked at me and said, "It's the beach guy." He went on to enthusiastically tell me that he still went to the beach in his head whenever he was beginning to get upset about anything.

You Always Have Options

I assure my clients that their decision to choose peace of mind over negative or upset reactions does not mean that they have no options. On the contrary, I tell them that they will be better able to express their wants and needs when they are calm and use the rational parts of their brains to find elegant solutions to challenging problems. Indeed, one of the most powerful things we can do is to maintain our cool and speak our truth even when we perceive that others are being irrational or unfair.

My son, Darqui, gave me many opportunities to practice going to the balcony during his first couple of years as a member of our family. Because he needed to recreate the chaos he had experienced before he joined our family, he would often say highly provocative things to us, such as "I hate you" or "You are the worst parents in the world." At first, the hurt that we experienced at these moments led us to respond with anger, which only served to escalate the intense emotions all of us were feeling.

It did not take us long to figure out that what we were doing was not working and that we needed to respond to Darqui more calmly and compassionately. When he said things to try to "push our buttons," we responded by telling him how much we loved him, that we would do anything we could to help him and that we were all in this together. Rather than fan the flames of his negative energy with our own reactivity, we absorbed it like a baseball being thrown into a big fluffy pillow (which is what I visualized as he told me what a terrible father I was).

We were surprised and relieved by how well our new strategy worked. Finally, we were able to turn conflicts that had once exhausted all of us into opportunities for deeper mutual understanding and dialogue. In fact, I once asked Darqui if he was testing us out to see if we would still love him regardless of the mean things he said to us during his emotional meltdowns. He replied, "Something like that." I then reassured him that he would be part of our family forever, regardless of how he behaved and that we would all benefit if he was secure enough to no longer need to test us out.

To develop the skills we need to stay calm even in the midst of highly challenging situations, it is important to practice not having a negative reaction to less significant events in our lives that we respond to with annoyance or frustration. Clearly, these emotions do not help us find our lost keys or clean up the trash after our dog has knocked it over. They take our focus away from solving the problem at hand and impair our quality of life.

Every time we choose happiness or peace of mind over a negative emotion, we rewire our brains to grease a quicker path to our balcony. Consequently, whenever we are faced with a very difficult challenge, we have the ability to instinctively detach from any reactivity we are experiencing and objectively review our options. Of course, this does not mean that we are going to feel serene when we are sitting in the emergency room with chest pains or involved in a traffic accident. However, we will be able to think more clearly and rationally in the midst of crisis situations and therefore respond more effectively.

Calm is Powerful

When faced with mistreatment by others, many people believe that they need to react with negative emotions to protect themselves. Clearly, this is appropriate in highly dangerous situations where an angry yell might save your life. However, it is also possible to very calmly inform others that their behavior is offensive or unfair. In fact, it is often more powerful to speak your truth in a civil manner than through angry words that others can easily dismiss by viewing you as irrational or out of control.

For example, I recently had an encounter with a man who began using the N-word in reference to President Obama as he changed my tire. Rather than respond with hostility, I calmly informed him that I was highly offended by his use of this word and asked him to apologize. When he refused, I informed him that I was going to get him fired from his company, which is exactly what happened shortly after this incident.

This man was clearly longing to engage me in a heated argument and, in fact, began to shout at me at one point during our exchange. However, my refusal to join him in the dance of anger left him bewildered and took all the wind out of his sails. Rather than rendering me powerless, my tempered response enabled me to defuse a volatile situation and left me feeling more rather than less powerful.

We also do not need anger or other negative emotions to eliminate unfairness, create loving communities or build a more just society. In fact, the men and women who have had the most positive impact on the world during my lifetime have all maintained a calm and compassionate demeanor as they fought for what they believed in. This eminent list includes Mahatma Gandhi, Martin Luther King, Jr., Eleanor Roosevelt, Nelson Mandela, President Obama, Mother Teresa and the Dalai Lama. All of these noble and powerful people radiated an inner sense of peace that helped them maintain their emotional strength and perspective in the midst of the obstacles they faced.

Although we may be able to protect ourselves or control others in the short run through our negative reactions, they do not help us in the long run to become our best selves, build healthy relationships or create the changes we want for ourselves. In fact, they are ultimately destructive because they stir up negative emotions in others, create conflict and drive others away from us.

The ability to move from reactivity to calm is a challenging task. As with any new skill, it takes a lot of practice to train ourselves to respond to difficult situations with composure and balance rather than frustration or anger. However, the results can be life-changing as we experience increasingly deeper levels of inner peace and consequently help to build a more peaceful world.

Try These Strategies on for Size

> ➤ Train yourself to respond to challenging situations effectively by detaching, "going to the balcony" and calmly deciding the best course of action.
> ➤ Recognize the visceral, physiological sensations you experience just before you have a negative reaction and make a strong commitment to not respond to them.
> ➤ Visualize a steel garage door slamming down and severing the connection between the challenging situation at hand and your emotional reaction to it.
> ➤ Recognize that no one can "make" you mad except yourself.
> ➤ Know that your choice to be calm and focused rather than emotionally reactive does not mean that you are powerless or do not have other options.

Chapter 10

APPRECIATE WHAT YOU HAVE

Most of us know that a major portal to happiness is to appreciate the good things in our lives. Whether we are marveling at the unconditional love our dogs give us, the comfort of pulling the blankets up to our neck on a cold winter's night or the joy of reconnecting to an old friend, our ability to bask in life's pleasures significantly improves the quality of our precious time on this Earth.

However, many people still live with an acute sense of what they lack rather than being grateful for all of the good things in their lives. They labor under the belief that they will be more fulfilled when they gain coveted possessions, achieve more professional success, and so on. Consequently, they live with a sense of scarcity rather than abundance.

Even when people get what they want, the satisfaction it brings them usually dims over time as the newness wears off and they set their sights on the next thing they believe will "make them" happy. Imagine that a lonely man finally finds a woman who provides him with companionship and love. Although initially ecstatic, he eventually begins to take what he has for granted and decides he can't be happy unless she gets a better job so they can buy a pool. I am sure you get the point - his assumption that he needs something else to be happy is the very thing that is preventing him from experiencing it.

It is much more self-compassionate to value what we already have in our lives even as we strive for further heights. For instance, we all can be thankful for the simple fact that we are alive. Although this may not sound like much, it sure beats the alternative as far as I am concerned. The privilege of life enables us to enjoy a good laugh, spend quality time with our loved ones and watch Monday Night Football. It also provides us with the opportunity to gain more wisdom and grow into the people we want to be.

I am always puzzled when people comment that life is short and wonder what they are comparing it to. Yes, some people's lives are tragically cut short. However, if we live a typical life span, we have around 16 hours a day, 365 days a year for 79 years (28,835 days) to appreciate everything good about our lives rather than what is lacking. Consequently, every day is like a feast and our sense of fulfillment enables us to feel like we are getting our just desserts.

Whenever I encounter people who appear to be very happy, I ask them what their secret is. They generally observe that they woke up that morning and/or have a lot to be thankful for. Their gratitude is a generous gift they give themselves and everyone they encounter because it enables them to experience "good cheer," which my best friend Carl believes is the secret to a happy life.

One of the happiest people I have ever known is my Aunt Jean. When I told her I was writing a book about how to achieve happiness through self-compassion, she began sending me lists of everything she loves about life such as spending time with her grandchildren and painting pictures of landscapes. I often read over her lists when I need to refill my own store of appreciation. Although she has certainly experienced many significant challenges in her life, none of them has even made a small dent in her ability to relish all that life has to offer.

A number of years ago, a host for the television show *60 Minutes* interviewed an older, African-American woman living in a hut in Mississippi for a story on poverty. Although she had no running water or other basic conveniences, she radiated joy and reported that she had everything she needed to be happy. A more recent story indicated that many of the richest people in the world are unhappy because they are not at the very top of the list. Without a doubt, our ability to appreciate what we have has a significant impact on our happiness and satisfaction with our lives.

In fact, if you want to prove to yourself how much control you have over your happiness, spend a few minutes thinking about everything that is lacking in your life. Very likely, you will feel a bit down. Now, switch your focus to everything for which you are grateful and your mood will likely lighten up significantly. I sometimes do this at 1-minute intervals, watching my mood bounce up and down like a yo-yo.

You can also use a gratitude meditation that I practice to fully appreciate all of the best things about my life. I take a deep breath in and then as I breathe out, I state something such as, "I have a happy family" or "Anita accepts me as I am." I generally list ten things I am grateful for and always enjoy a deep sense of satisfaction as a result. I also frequently remind myself of my favorite simple pleasures, such as sitting in my hot tub on a chilly morning, the taste of Cajun catfish or the beauty of the sun shining down on the Buddha statue sitting peacefully in my front yard.

I often ask my depressed clients to list five things that they appreciate. I relish seeing their spirits lighten as they focus on what they are grateful for and consequently develop a more positive perspective on their lives. I also encourage my clients to bathe themselves in gratitude in between our sessions like it is water cascading down over them from a waterfall.

It is ironic that people who deeply appreciate what they have in their lives have often experienced past difficulties that have provided them with a valuable sense of perspective. For example, Darqui suffered from a very difficult childhood, which included being moved around from foster home to foster home, living in a shelter for over a year and often going hungry. In fact, he remembers eating paper to fill up the hole in his stomach. No one would question why if he only focused on the trauma of his early years rather than the good things he has experienced.

However, Darqui appreciates what he has more than anyone I have ever known, which makes being his father such a joyful and meaningful experience. I doubt many fathers get a big hug and hear the words, "I love you," from their teenage sons upon receiving a new toothbrush, but these are gifts Darqui gives out generously. He also frequently proclaims that any given day is the best one of his life and has never once complained about what he doesn't have.

It may be that Darqui was born with the ability to relish what he has, but I think this is highly unlikely. From his perspective, any day where he is not in physical danger or has enough food to eat is a good one. In fact, if I ever worry that Anita and I are not sufficiently providing for his needs, he always reassures me by saying, "Don't worry about it. I know what it is like to not have anything."

With Darqui's help, I strive to be mindful of everything I am thankful for. When I fall into the trap of thinking about what I don't have or haven't accomplished, I am relieved to remember that I always have the option to shift my focus to all of the things that are great about my life. Whenever I make this choice, I am rewarded with a welcome burst of appreciation and happiness. I wish the same for you.

<u>Try These Strategies on for Size</u>

➢ Recognize that we impair our happiness when we always look for something else to happen in our lives to achieve it.

➢ Value and savor all of the good things in your life and live with a sense of abundance rather than scarcity.

➢ Prove to yourself how much control you have over your happiness by thinking about everything lacking in your life, switching your focus to everything for which you are grateful and then noticing how this exercise changes your mood.

➢ Appreciate the positive things in your life by listing them as you breathe out.

Chapter 11

ENJOY THE PRESENT MOMENT

Although most people would agree that it's better to enjoy the moment than to ruminate about our past difficulties, current problems or future worries, it can be difficult to do this for a variety of reasons. One is that most of us were not taught this crucial skill by our parents or in school, outside of a small number of schools that teach mindfulness. Another is that we are socialized to believe that our worth is based on our accomplishments, social status, etc., and we fear that we will not reach our goals unless we are moving full-speed ahead at all times.

Finally, the biggest obstacle to being happy and peaceful in the present moment is our mind. Although our mind is useful in many ways, such as helping us solve complex problems or remember important information, it also is the source of the unhelpful thoughts and judgments that create most of our unhappiness. Therefore, the more we identify with our minds, the more emotional pain we experience.

This pain magically disappears when you transcend your mind and simply focus on the pleasures or meaning of the present moment. As Bruce Springsteen (one of my heroes) sings in his classic song, "Thunder Road," "You can hide beneath your covers and study your pain." However, he encourages you to instead venture forth into the wonders of the moment and "Roll down the windows and let the wind blow back your hair."

Our problems exist largely within our minds and are consequently only as real as we make them. This is not to say that we do not sometimes face serious challenges in our lives that we need to take action to overcome, if we can. However, our success in changing any life situation is contingent on what we do rather than how much we define it as a problem or ruminate about it. At the risk of sounding a bit simplistic, unhappy people spend their time thinking about their problems and happy people focus on solving them or transcending them by simply being present.

The Power of Now

Eckhart Tolle writes about the process of shifting from our minds to the moment in his uplifting book, *The Power of Now*. He states, "As soon as you honor the present moment, all unhappiness and struggle dissolve, and life begins to flow with joy and ease." He also reminds us that the past and future do not exist outside of our minds. Finally, he advises us to free ourselves from the grip of our minds by embracing rather than resisting the now and then deciding whether we need to take any action to change it.

When I first read *The Power of Now*, I so strongly identified with my mind that I had a difficult time grasping what Tolle was encouraging us to do. I read certain sentences over and over as I pondered how I could enter the now. I eventually realized that the only thing I needed to do was to stop thinking about what I needed to do and there I was: in the moment. In fact, this is the only place I have ever been and was just too caught up in my thoughts to know it. What a simple and profound truth!

Highly cerebral people who have been able to use their powerful minds to develop new ideas and achieve a high level of professional success often struggle to enjoy the moment because they overvalue thinking at the expense of being. Consequently, when they experience unhappiness, they analyze why they are unhappy, which drives them deeper into the realm of thought and further away from whatever possible pleasures the present moment has to offer.

In contrast, my daughter, Nikki, savors the moment as well as anyone I have ever known. Whether enjoying her favorite foods, gazing at the fire in our fireplace or listening to the birds at our family cabin, she almost always has a look of satisfaction and peace on her face. It is unfortunate that many people are unable to see beyond her cognitive challenges and recognize how much she has to teach all of us about being in the moment and simply enjoying life, with no judgments, concern for the past or worries about the future.

Portals to the Present

There are a variety of portals into the moment that are accessible to everyone. One is to switch our focus from our thoughts to what we are experiencing through our senses, which opens up an entirely new world from the one we experience when we limit our reality to simply what is going on inside our heads. Whether we enter this world through eating fresh blueberries, actually smelling the roses or listening to Beethoven's 7th symphony (my favorite), we experience the gifts the present moment has to offer.

I recently worked with a client who exhausted himself by obsessing about all of his perceived shortcomings. I asked him to try an experiment by thinking intently about one thing he did not like about himself and then quickly switching his focus to looking at the trees outside my office window and watching the leaves swaying in the wind. He was amazed by his immediate sense of greater inner peace as he left the world of his mind and ventured into the moment. I reminded him as he left our session that he always had the capacity to change his focus from the torments of his mind to the rewards that each moment has to offer.

In fact, I routinely encourage my clients not to think about their problems as they drive away from my office. I advise them to instead focus all of their attention on what they are experiencing through their senses as they listen to music, notice the world around them or simply feel their hands on the steering wheel. The greater peace and presence they experience provides them with a much needed emotional lift and an opening to an inviting world which exists beyond their troubles.

Lose Yourself in the "Flow"

We can also "lose ourselves" in an activity that so fully captures our attention that we leave the realm of thought. When we are in this place, which is often referred to as "flow," we transcend our worries and our awareness of time. We are totally immersed in the moment and operate from the most expansive and creative parts of ourselves. The happiest people I know maximize their opportunities to pursue their passions within this wonderful state, which is one of the best antidotes to boredom and depression.

Whenever I am working with clients who have difficulty enjoying the moment, I ask them to identify activities that enable them to get outside of their heads and into this sense of "flow." Frequently mentioned activities include gardening, reading or watching a captivating movie. I then discuss with them how they can rearrange their lives so they can spend more time doing whatever brings "flow" into their lives.

Bruce Springsteen validated the power of "flow" when he noted in a 2012 *New Yorker* article that his early concerts would go on for many hours because they provided him with his only opportunity to leave the demons in his mind behind. Unfortunately for both Springsteen and his adoring fans, his concerts eventually had to end.

Thirdly, we can view the moments of our lives as opportunities to be savored rather than stepping stones to the achievement of our goals. Clearly, life is not a race to some distant finish line and when we die, I highly doubt that we are met by some entity with a clipboard that lists what we did not accomplish. Indeed, happy people focus on being as much as doing and use their precious time on this planet to enjoy the present moment rather than simply getting things done.

I love to watch children at play because they are generally so much better than adults at being present and having fun. Whether they are making up a new game, building a sand castle at the beach or just chasing each other around, their glee is infectious. I wish every adult had the ability to be as playful and spontaneous as they were when they were 6 years old.

Find Serenity Through Meditation

Finally, meditation provides us with an excellent portal to leave the tyranny of our thoughts and enjoy the present moment. Although I am not an expert in this time-honored practice, I have experimented with many different types of meditation over the past 40 years and cherish the inner peace and stillness it brings me.

I begin by breathing deeply, which helps me relax and get out of my thoughts, slow down my physiology and remain attentive to whatever sensations I am experiencing within my body. I then visualize that I am taking an elevator down deep within my psyche to a place filled with expansive, white light. When I am able to remain in this place for an extended period of time, I experience a profound sense of serenity that fills my entire being.

When I first began to experience inner peace through meditation, I used to fear that I had gone in too deep, never to return to the outside world. This caused me to jolt myself out of my bliss. I now know that I have nothing to fear and would actually be content to spend the rest of my life in this wonderful place, although this would certainly cause my mail to pile up and my beloved bulldog, Gus, to go hungry.

The main obstacle to the meditative peace I crave is the thought that there is some way I *should* be feeling that I am not, which blocks my ability to actually be in the moment. The best way for me to rid myself of these judgments is to visualize that they are floating away from my consciousness like released balloons. I am then completely free to be aware of whatever is happening in the moment with acceptance and appreciation.

I encourage most of my clients to meditate and often practice it with them during our sessions. In fact, the power of meditation to find inner peace was illustrated in the experience of a client who suffered from such severe anxiety that making it through each day was like climbing up a steep mountain. However, at the end of one of our joint meditations, he happily reported that he had finally transcended the thoughts that had bedeviled him for most of his life and experienced a peaceful place within that he described as "underneath" his anxiety.

One of the major challenges my clients face when they begin meditating is that as soon as they try to quiet their thoughts, the "noise" in their heads gets louder, as if their thoughts are feeling neglected and demanding more attention. However, this period of heightened mental activity usually only lasts for a brief period of time as long as we focus on entering a deeper and quieter place within. Fortunately, the meditative process usually becomes easier each time we go through it and learn our path to tranquility.

Along with the traditional meditation I practice, I often stop whatever I am doing during my generally busy days, take a couple of deep breaths and enter the place within where my inner peace patiently awaits me. This helps me recalibrate my energy to a slower frequency and more fully relish the present moment. When I return to the outside world, I always feel refreshed and more centered.

An excellent place to practice brief meditations is when you are stopped at a red light. If you are on the way to the hospital to give birth or running late to your wedding, this is probably impossible. In less urgent situations, however, there is no reason to be impatient at red lights. You might as well relax, breathe deeply and enter a peaceful place within, which is as available to you at that moment as it is when you are sitting on a warm, tropical beach. Vacations are great, but why not enjoy a peaceful moment in the middle of a dreary winter day while waiting for the light to finally turn green?

Although the concept of meditation might sound too complex for children to grasp, I have found that they are better at it than most adults with whom I work, who are too caught up in their heads to find their peaceful place within. This was illustrated to me during a recent training I conducted for 3rd and 4th graders on being compassionate to yourself and others. I gave them the opportunity to meditate for 5 minutes and encouraged them to leave the reality of the outside world and plunge deep into their inner selves. They immediately found a comfortable place to lie down on their classroom floor and the room was filled with silence.

When I subsequently asked them where their journey had taken them, their answers were magical. One boy noted that he had been in a beautiful meadow filled with butterflies and flowers and a girl described her experience sitting on the top of a cloud as it drifted across the sky. I was struck by how easily children use their imagination to find a peaceful place within in contrast to most adults who are too burdened by their responsibilities and worries to journey into their inner selves.

It is often difficult for people who have experienced significant trauma to enjoy the present moment because their neurological systems have been wired to be on the alert for possible danger. Consequently, they tend to overthink everything and are hyper-vigilant to any real or perceived threats. They fear that if they relax and relish the moment, they will not be able to adequately protect themselves.

The impact of childhood trauma was illustrated to me in my work with Tanya, who grew up in a chaotic and violent household. From an early age, she took on the responsibility of trying to keep the peace between her drug-addicted parents and take care of her younger sister. Not surprisingly, she became a highly anxious and overly responsible adult who always put her own needs aside to take care of her children and support her family. The only time she was able to escape her worries was when she was under the influence of alcohol, as is the case with many survivors of trauma.

When I asked her if she had ever been able to simply relax and enjoy the moment, Tanya looked at me as if I had asked her if we could have our next session on the moon. She explained that she could not afford to take the risk of letting her worry go because it might result in something terrible happening. I assured her that her anxiety did not prevent bad things from happening and that she did not need it to effectively protect and provide for herself and her family. I also encouraged Tanya to take the risk of letting go of her hyper-vigilance to prove to herself that it was not serving her in any way.

Over time, Tanya was finally able to let go of her anxiety without the help of alcohol and surprised herself by developing a previously unknown sense of inner peace. She was relieved to discover that she actually functioned better when her mind wasn't going around in endless circles. Rather than spend our entire session talking about her fears, we began to focus mainly on what she was doing to relish each moment and ended each session with at least 10 minutes of meditation. I shared her deep satisfaction that she had finally put the fallout from her traumatic childhood behind her and learned how to more fully enjoy each moment.

Surrender to What Is

Many people are unable to enjoy the present moment because they are preoccupied with negative emotions about the reality of their lives, the way other people behave or the world around them. Rather than surrendering to what is, they are upset about it and yearn for things to be different, which accomplishes nothing except causing them to experience frustration. In fact, the inability to accept reality is one of the major causes of human unhappiness.

For instance, if your wallet is stolen, you can focus on being angry with the person who stole it or yourself for not being more careful with it. You may also remember all of the other times you have been treated unfairly and work yourself into a lather of negative emotions that does not accomplish anything. It is much more self-compassionate for you to accept the fact that your wallet is gone, make a mental note about how to better protect it in the future, cancel your stolen credit cards and do something special for yourself to revive your spirit.

For most of my life, I resisted the concept of surrendering to whatever reality I faced and hated the term "it is what it is" because I believed it meant that I needed to accept things that were not right rather than try to change them. I viewed acceptance as a "cop out" from my responsibility to make the world a better place or become the best person I could be. I mistakenly believed that resisting reality would somehow make it different.

Fortunately, I have learned experientially that surrendering to what is does not prevent me from doing whatever I need to improve my life circumstances, take better care of myself or be helpful to others. It simply enables me to focus all of my energy on whatever I need to do rather than wasting it on feeling frustrated or upset.

In fact, whenever my ability to enjoy the moment is impaired by my worry about a challenging situation I face or might face in the future, I ask myself a simple question, "Can I do anything about this situation?" If I can do something about it at that moment, I do it. If I can do something about it in the future, I plan out when and how I will do it. If there is nothing I can do to change whatever is worrying me, I accept this fact and let the worry go.

When I am working with clients who are unhappy about a difficult situation they are unable to change, I encourage them to try to stop thinking about it and simply be present in the moment through the use of the portals I have discussed in this chapter. This appears to be a daunting challenge for most of my clients, particularly if they are in the habit of ruminating about their problems. However, the happiness and inner peace they experience when they are able to be in the moment even for a brief instant motivates them to figure out how to stay in this inviting place for longer periods of time.

I once worked with Sam, who was very upset that his fiancée had broken up with him. When we first began our sessions together, he spent most of his energy trying to figure out how he could get her back. However, when his fiancée did not respond to his repeated e-mails, he realized that she had no interest in getting back with him and that he had no choice but to accept this painful fact. I consequently encouraged him to visualize that he was banging his head against a brick wall every time he thought about his fiancée and focus instead on enjoying each moment and throwing himself into activities he loved such as playing in his rock band and camping. After he stopped trying to change what was, he was surprised by how quickly he recovered from his loss.

I hope you too are able to get out of your head, live more fully in the present moment and surrender to what is. A rich world awaits you!

Try These Strategies on for Size

- ➤ Recognize that your problems exist mainly within your mind and transcend them by focusing on the present moment.
- ➤ Switch your attention from your thoughts to what you are experiencing through your senses.
- ➤ "Lose" yourself in activities that so fully capture your attention that you leave the realm of thought.
- ➤ Relish all of the moments of your life rather than simply viewing them as opportunities to get things done.
- ➤ Develop a regular meditation practice that enables you to experience a deep sense of inner peace and fulfillment.
- ➤ Practice brief meditations whenever you need to more fully relish the present moment.
- ➤ Surrender to what is rather than resisting it and know that this does not prevent you from taking whatever actions you can to create the changes you want in yourself or the world.
- ➤ Take the risk of letting go of your hyper-vigilance to prove that you do not need it to protect yourself.
- ➤ Whenever you are caught up in worrying, ask yourself if there is something you can do about what you are worrying about. If there is, do it. If there is nothing you can do, let your worry go.

Chapter 12
PASS ON YOUR COMPASSION TO OTHERS

One of the best things about achieving self-compassion is that it enables us to have more compassion for others. As a result, we are compelled to do what we can for our fellow human beings and build a better world by working to eliminate suffering and injustice.

Highly self-compassionate people give off an aura of peace and happiness that is infectious. Dr. Howard Cutler, who co-authored *The Art of Happiness* with the Dalai Lama, described their attendance at a dinner for high-powered lawmakers in Washington, D.C. He observed that most of the guests were tense and competitive as they tried to impress each other with their importance and make connections that would benefit them politically. Rather than get caught up in all of the posturing going on around him, the Dalai Lama sat in the corner in his simple robe, beaming happily at everyone.

Dr. Cutler noticed that two lawmakers who sat down next to the Dalai Lama had a very different demeanor. They were relaxed and smiling as they held the Dalai Lama's hand. Gradually, the group around the Dalai Lama grew larger as more people chose to bask in love and compassion rather than jockeying for power. Just imagine if we all had the ability of the Dalai Lama to bring out the best in everyone around us. World peace would break out and we would all benefit from being members of a more caring and compassionate human community.

Although the Dalai Lama is an exceptional person, we all share his capacity to make a positive impact on everyone we encounter through our happiness and peace of mind. As we act on this capacity, we inspire others to do so as well. As Marianne Williamson writes in *A Return to Love: Reflections on the Principles of a Course in Miracles,* "And as we let our own light shine, we unconsciously give other people permission to do the same. As we are liberated from our own fear, our presence automatically liberates others."

Some people take great care of themselves and never trample on the rights of others and yet choose - for whatever reason - to invest little or no energy in helping others. Although they may feel content with their lives, they are depriving themselves of the deep satisfaction they could experience by extending emotional support to a friend in need, standing up for what they know is right or fighting for worthy causes. Unfortunately, they are missing out on one of the best aspects of life.

My ability to treat myself with self-compassion has enabled me to be a more giving and loving person. It has also provided me with increased energy and passion to fight for the causes I most deeply believe in, including eliminating racism, bullying, homophobia, social injustice and all forms of prejudice, including towards people who have cognitive challenges such as my daughter, Nikki. In fact, I wish I could wave a magic wand and create a world where Nikki, and everyone like her, are viewed as the perfect beings they are.

However, I never forget to refuel and recharge by treating myself with the same compassion I always try to extend to others. I hope you too are able to achieve the happiness, peace and presence of self-compassion that will be your gift to yourself and the world - you deserve it!

Printed in the United States
By Bookmasters